LIFE W

I MAY HAVE CROHN'S DISEASE, BUT IT DOESN'T HAVE ME

LORRAINE HUNTLEY

Edwardsville, IL

LIFE WITHOUT LIMITS
I MAY HAVE CROHN'S DISEASE BUT IT DOESN'T HAVE ME
Lorraine Huntley

Cover photo courtesy of: John Ridgeway of Ridgeway Portrait Design, Maryville, IL.

Copyright © 2014 by Lorraine Huntley
All rights reserved.

No part of this publication may be reproduced, stored in a retrieval system, distributed or transmitted in any form or by any means, including photocopying, recording, scanning, or other electronic or mechanical methods, except as permitted under Section 107 or 108 of the 1976 United States Copyright Act, without the prior written permission of the publisher.

Limit of Liability/Disclaimer of Warranty: While the publisher and author have used their best efforts in preparing this book, they make no representations or warranties with respect to the accuracy or completeness of the contents of this book and specifically disclaim an implied warranties of merchantability or fitness for a particular purpose. No warranty may be created or extended by sales representatives or written sales materials. The advice and strategies contained herein may not be suitable for your situation. You should consult with a professional where appropriate. Neither the publisher nor author shall be liable for any loss of profit or any other commercial damages, including but not limited to special, incidental, consequential or other damages.

Library of Congress Cataloging - in - Publication Data is available upon request.

ISBN: 9781500539818

For those battling with chronic illness;

*and for my husband Mark,
and daughter Tah-Wah.*

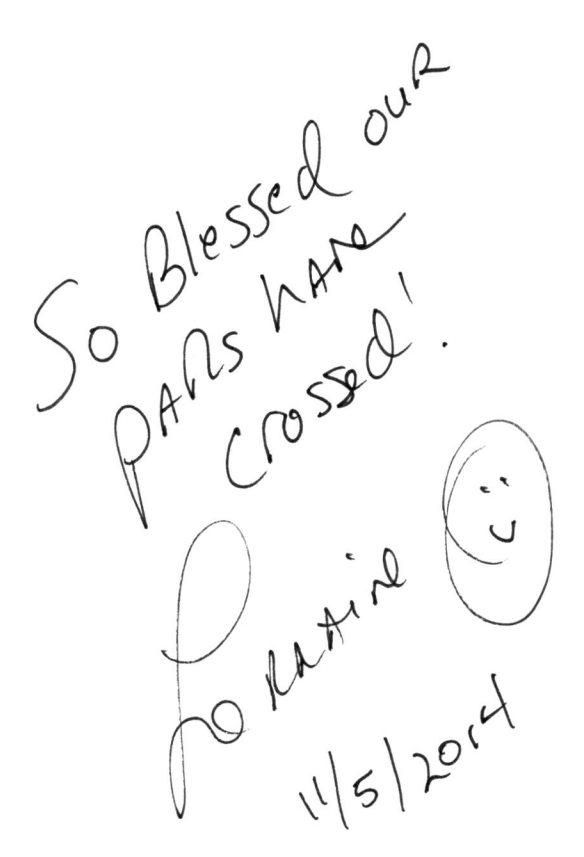

So Blessed our paths have crossed!

Lorraine 😊

11/5/2014

If it doesn't challenge you, it doesn't change you!

Table of Contents

Author's Note

ONE: Where do I begin? ☆ 1

TWO: Family Time ☆ 9

THREE: Dance, Prance and Pose ☆ 19

FOUR: Dance like no one - or everyone - is watching ☆21

FIVE: School time, dear oh golden rule time ☆ 37

SIX: Time to jazz it up a bit ☆ 41

SEVEN: Where the story begins ☆ 51

EIGHT: Now the story really begins ☆ 57

NINE: Gotta get, Gotta get, Gotta get your SeaLegs ☆ 69

TEN: On to the next show ☆ 81

ELEVEN: What comes next? ☆ 95

TWELVE: Ding Dong, bells are ringing ☆ 103

THIRTEEN: Where do I go from here? ☆ 111

FOURTEEN: Time to make the move ☆ 117

FIFTEEN: Changes ☆ 133

SIXTEEN: College Bound ☆ 143

SEVENTEEN: Ten years later ☆ 153

EIGHTEEN: The classes that mattered ☆ 157

NINETEEN: The end of an Era ☆ 167

TWENTY: Moving on to my last semester ☆ 171

TWENTY-ONE: School doesn't teach what you need to know: My most beneficial learning ☆ 177

TWENTY-TWO: Finally, I get to do what I have worked for ☆ 189

TWENTY-THREE: My time as a clinical dietitian ☆ 197

TWENTY-FOUR: Moving on to what I *want* to do, not what I *have* to do ☆ 211

TWENTY-FIVE: Good times, not so good times ☆ 227

TWENTY-SIX: Turning the Big 4-0! ☆ 233

TWENTY-SEVEN: The non-traditional student ☆ 243

TWENTY-EIGHT: One year down and one to go ☆ 251

TWENTY-NINE: Many new ventures ☆ 257

THIRTY: What the heck was I thinking? ☆ 269

THIRTY ONE: Oh, when will I ever learn? ☆ 285

THIRTY TWO: Travels, New carrots and …. ☆ 293

THIRTY THREE: My Crohn's treatments ☆ 307

THIRTY FOUR: Five-year anniversary ☆ 317

THIRTY FIVE: Oh, the things clients say! ☆ 323

THIRTY SIX: Where do I go from here? ☆ 331

THIRTY-SEVEN: The end of my best run ☆ 341

THIRTY-EIGHT: The chapter I just couldn't write ☆ 343

THIRTY-NINE: Crohn's Disease: Defining and Managing ☆ 349

Resources ☆ 360

Acknowledgements ☆ 361

AUTHOR'S NOTE

In order to pen this book, I relied upon my journals, my memories, and I consulted with friends and family to help me accurately recall dates, times and events. I have changed some names and tried not to purposely identify any one particular person.

I have been told on numerous occasions, "write the book that is in your head." I never really knew I had that much information to share about my journey or myself, but after thinking long and hard, I realized I did have many stories and challenges that I have faced over the years, which might be worth sharing. So here I sit putting *pen to paper*.

Imagine you are standing on stage dressed in a bedazzled bikini, wearing high-heeled stilettos and a giant feathery headdress. The lights are out in the theater, but you can hear the audience waiting for the curtain to go up. You are nervous; all your years of training and rehearsing are finally culminating in this one super emotionally charged moment. You are sure you are going to forget the dance routine; you are sure you didn't preset your costumes; you are sure your makeup isn't dark enough. And then, with your heart pounding, you hear the promoter say: "Ladies and Gentlemen, welcome to the show. Sit back, relax and enjoy the performance by the Jean Ann Ryan dancers. And now (as the curtain goes up), here they are."

I never in a million years would have dreamt that I would dance on a cruise ship in the skimpiest costumes I had ever seen; travel throughout the Caribbean, and see the world. I was basically getting paid to do what I loved doing most: DANCE. I also never imagined that I would, or could, run a 5K - let alone a marathon - and I certainly never would have guessed that I would have a successful career in the nutrition and fitness business. Even though I never expected to be diagnosed with an incurable disease, it is ultimately that disease that has made me who I am. I might have Crohn's disease, but it does not have me.

Anyone who knows me knows that I have ungodly long fingernails, which I polish in the most obnoxious colors. People ask, "How do you type?", "How do you get dressed?" "How do you...?" Well, I answer, "No differently than you"! You see, we really are all alike - we just come wrapped in different packages with different ribbons and bows. Underneath and inside, we all possess the same cells, bones, muscles and senses. It is how we present these qualities that set us apart.

I am not really certain how to write a book. I have never written one, so I do not really know where to begin. I am not sure just how much information is too much or how much is not enough. I have never been one to leave people guessing as to which side of the fence I am on. You pretty much know where you stand with me. There is very little gray in my world and lots of black or white, yes or no, right or wrong. Either it is or it is not; either you are or you are not. Do not give me an excuse, a why or a because: those answers do not fly with me. Maybe that has something to do with being a Gemini; you know, right brain/left brain, good/bad, yin/yang. I am hot or cold, happy or sad, training 200 percent for an event or not at all (well, that never really happens). Is this is a good thing? Being so focused, so driven? Shouldn't you always have some sort of moderation or middle ground? The saying goes, "Everything in moderation." But I have always struggled to find that gray area, some happy medium. I realize the older I get that I do not need to tackle life at warp speed, and I have found that sometimes, yes sometimes, less IS more. That, my friend, has taken me every bit of 25-plus years to come to terms with, let alone verbalize. So, maybe I do have lots of stories to share; maybe I do have some drive, dedication and determination that will help you through a tough time. Maybe I am supposed to write this book that is in my head. So, without any further ado, here I go.

ONE

WHERE DO I BEGIN?

Honestly, when I hear about some of the trials and tribulations, and battles and fights amongst siblings I am glad to be an only child. I never thought it to be a lonely existence. I never wished I had a brother or a sister. I never knew any differently. Being an only child was the way it was.

I grew up in Boca Raton, Florida and lived on a street with at least 25 kids around my age. We would swim, play kickball and ride our bikes all over the neighborhood. Most of us all went to the same school and our weekends were filled with fun and games. Back in the early '70s, times were different. You could go anywhere on your bike and you could play outside until the street lights came on. We weren't a mischievous group, but we did have fun.

I did have my biking limits and one summer day I clearly remember going well beyond that limit. My mom and dad were not home, it was a sunny weekend day, and we wanted to ride. You see, there was this road - Camino Real - that had three small bridges and if you went fast enough over the bridge on your bike you could become airborne (I later realized you could do this in your car, too). You know, the kind of airborne that makes your stomach jump into your throat! Well, this one particular day I did go airborne only to land sideways and crash to the ground; skid a long way and tear the living heck out of my ankle. I was crying, bleeding and my friends were screaming.

My injury was so bad you could see the talus bone (the one on the top of your ankle). My friends scooped me up, propped me on their handlebars and we raced back home. I think we left my bike in the street somewhere, but I really do not remember. Once back at my friend's house, they placed me in a bathtub full of water. There was blood gushing everywhere and we literally watched my ankle swell to the size of a grapefruit. I likely should have gone to the ER, but then I really would have gotten into trouble, plus none of us were old enough to drive. So, my friends cleaned up the road rash, bandaged me as tightly as they could and I hobbled home. I limped for weeks, and yes, got into tons of trouble, especially since I took dance classes and the injury made dancing a little difficult.

How is it when your parents say, "We will find out anyway," they always do? You never learn that lesson until you become a parent yourself. We all think we can get away with it, and no one will find out. It's a breeze, so let's try it. But always, lo and behold, parents find out. They just know. And then, there is always hell to pay!

The streets in South Florida were paved with tar and that meant in the heat of the day you could see the steam rising from them. And if you have ever been to South Florida, then you know that every day at about 3 p.m., it rains for five short minutes. That is it, just a quick shower, but enough that the heat and humidity cause the roads to steam, and when the roads steam that means the pavement is HOT.

We rarely wore shoes when we played kickball. I remember one day, the pavement was so hot, we all must have looked like we were jumping around on hot coals. Needless to say, I burnt the bottom of both of my feet. It took a few weeks to heal, again, not a good thing when you take dance classes. This was yet another lesson learned the hard way.

Now, do not think I am only going to tell you about injuries and pain. There were many happy and fun times, too. With so many kids on the block we had a ton of fun together and to this day I still keep in touch with many of them.

One of my favorite memories was getting in the car with my friend, Betsy, at 4 a.m. We had our pillows in hand and would climb into the backseat, snuggle in and sleep as my mom and dad drove us to Disney World (aka The Magic Kingdom) in Orlando which opened in October of 1971. It was a long four-hour drive, but if we left early we could arrive when the park opened. Back in the early days there was only the Magic Kingdom: no Epcot, no Universal Studios, no Animal Kingdom, no Hollywood Studios - you could see the entire park and ride all the rides in one day.

When we arrived, daddy always parked in the "Pluto" parking lot and we took the shuttle to the main gate. I remember walking through the gates and seeing "Main Street USA" in front of me. Wow, there it was: so big, and so pretty. We would plan our course of action; Frontierland, Tomorrowland, Adventureland, Fantasyland, and finally Liberty Square. We would run to the first "land" on our itinerary and get in line so we could ride our favorite ride.

Back when the park first opened there was no such thing as a FastPass; you actually had to wait in line AND you had to give the attendants an actual ticket. There were "A," "B," "C," "D" or "E" tickets available. The best rides such as It's a Small World, the Haunted

Mansion or Space Mountain were considered the "A" rides and you only got five "A" tickets. We always rode those rides first and then worked our way to the less desirable "E" ticket rides. There we were with our Mickey Mouse ears waiting in line in the hot summer sun and loving every minute of it.

At the end of the day, we would enjoy dinner in Cinderella's castle and then watch the midnight parade with all the lights, floats and Disney characters. I can still picture Betsy and I standing there with our mouths wide open, clapping our hands and hoping that one of the princesses would see us and blow a kiss our way.

When the parade was over, we would shuttle back to our car and drive home, singing the theme song from It's A Small World After All, eventually falling asleep and dreaming of sugar plum fairies and princes. We used to make this trip two or three times a year. It never got old; and we always managed to make each trip different and memorable. I am pretty sure somewhere - packed away for safekeeping - I have an original Magic Kingdom map and a ticket booklet, or at least a ticket or two.

Aside from all the fun and games we had, there was still the usual business of school and homework. I attended a Catholic grade school - St Joan of Arc - which was only a few miles from home, but too far to walk. My first grade teacher was Sister Pious. She was the dearest, kindest, quietest, most special soul I had ever met. She was a great teacher and I thoroughly enjoyed learning from her. I did get in trouble quite a bit. It seems I had the gift of gab, and I had trouble sitting still for long periods of time. But, the consequence of misbehaving in a Catholic school was, as we all know, the dreaded ruler. Sister Pious never used the ruler to reprimand us - that punishment was left for Sr. Delourdes, our third grade teacher. She was not the dearest, kindest, quietest, most special soul I had ever met. In fact, she was a flat out mean and frustrated woman. I learned to keep my mouth closed in her class, but, yes, somehow I still managed to get my hands smacked with that ruler!

Grade school was a fun time with about 20 to 30 kids in each grade. We were all pretty close and got along pretty well. I clearly remember one day in the 5th or 6th grade when the weather was actually cold!! Not cool, but cold! We did own a few sweaters and light jackets, but we never really wore them. However, one morning the sky was an odd color and very thick looking. As we were sitting in our classroom learning and looking out the windows, the next thing we knew there were snowflakes falling from the sky. What was this strange sight? We knew it was snow, but really? It was South Florida! It is not supposed to snow here. We were allowed to go outside and experience this strange phenomenon. We ran around trying to catch these little white flakes on our tongue. We must have looked like goofballs with our tongues sticking out and our arms flailing as we ran around the school grounds. Needless to say, the snow event was short lived and that was the only time I remember it ever snowing (and I'm using that term loosely) in South Florida.

South Florida was green all year round. Most of our trees were palms or pines, and they do not shed like the leaves of an oak or maple tree does. We always thought it was a hoot to send a Christmas card with a picture of a cardboard Santa propped up in the backyard while we were lounging in a bathing suit! How taunting and torturous it must have been for our fellow family members, who lived up north, to see us happy and warm on Christmas Day. Now, after many years of living in the Midwest, I would not have been so amused to receive one of these cards, but at the time it seemed like a great idea!

Amongst having lots of neighborhood and school friends in Boca, I also had lots of family in South Florida and we would all get together for holidays, birthdays, picnics and beach bumming. I loved all the fun and sunny things there were to do. I used to live for the beach on a Saturday morning. Nothing was better than tanning between 10 a.m. and 2 p.m. with the iodine bottle and a reflective panel. There was little concern of skin cancer, as there was not the awareness there is today, so we would lay on the beach, listen to the waves, and listen to our skin sizzle.

One of my favorite ocean memories is when my parents and I would sit on the beach and see how many boats we could find. I always seemed to win. Better eyesight? Or did they just let me win?

I liked to walk up and down the beach and pick shells, but swimming was what I enjoyed most. That was until Steven Spielberg ruined it for me when the movie "Jaws" was released! I went to the theater to see this movie, and was scared to death! As a result, I did not go in the ocean for many years. I would barely get my feet wet for fear that Jaws was lurking nearby. I shake my fist at you Mr. Spielberg for taking away some of my best beach years.

It was not until we took a trip to California and visited Universal Studios where I saw the robotically controlled, fairly small, shark that scared the daylights out of me, and then I became really mad. *THAT* is what I had been afraid of all these years! Really!

TWO

FAMILY TIME

I come from quite a large family as my mom had 13 brothers and sisters, and my dad had eight. As a child, all of my mom's brothers and sisters were alive, while my dad had a brother who died in the war and a sister who died at a young age. Most of the extended family lived up North or out West, which gave us many places to go to and visit. To this day I cannot even begin to count the number of 1st, 2nd, 3rd or even 4th cousins that are in my family. We did have a few family reunions, but the only one I attended was in the early 1970s. At that time there were approximately 125 family members, so if we had another reunion today, oh my, you do the math. I would not even begin to be able to count them all. Maybe that is why I am an only child.

Anyway, like I said we all traveled and visited each other in the traditional sense of getting on a plane or driving to another city, but one day my daddy's dead brother decided to visit me. I had seen him in pictures wearing his military uniform - very handsome, very Italian looking, but I never expected to see him walking through our living room in a dinner jacket! I saw a ghost! The weird thing was that I was not scared.

My mom, aunt and I were playing cards at the kitchen table and my seat was situated so I could see into the living room, and down the hallway. During our game, I apparently saw something out of the corner of my eye, turned to look and then turned pale white. My mom and aunt asked what I was looking at, and when I told them it was Uncle Ray (Daddy's dead brother) they started crying. They did not ask me if I was making it up, or tell me I was mistaken. They just cried. Maybe they had seen him before or maybe they wanted to see him. I remember he looked peaceful, like he was on a mission as he walked through the house. I guess he just disappeared into thin air. I don't really remember. They say people who die before their time often wander around in the physical world searching for a way to cross over to the "other side."

I do remember the experience got me thinking about ghosts and spirits, and if there is such a thing as an afterlife. Being raised as a Catholic, we were taught not to believe in reincarnation, but something has always made me wonder if there was more out there. We could not possibly be here for such a short period of time. I remember I always seemed to "know" things; I seemed to know there was something else out there. This gi-nor-mous solar system cannot just contain the intelligent life of planet Earth, can it? How do you explain deja-vu?

I have always had this uncanny ability to know the answers to questions, to be able to say the right things at the right time, to just know what to do; even when I was a little girl. My aunt May who lived in Pittsburgh liked to have her fortune or palm read, and one day she asked her psychic if she would do a reading about me. She gave her a picture of me and told her my date of birth and the psychic told her I was an old soul, a sage of sorts. I was wise beyond my years. I have lived many times and for many years. I would be a teacher and I loved movement.

I also had my date of birth analyzed using numerology, which further confirmed I was an old soul, had learned many lessons and only had a few lessons left to master. *Hmm, what the heck does that mean?* I did not know, it is just what the readings revealed.

Another strange childhood memory I have is of a recurring dream. The dream took place in this forest-like area. It was of me lying on the bottom of a lake. I was dead. I had drowned. It was (best as I can figure) upstate New York, based on the forest-like trees and scenery. I would have this same dream over and over: always the same, always seeing myself lying there – dead. Surprisingly I was not afraid of what I saw and today I am not afraid of the water (well until that damn Jaws movie). I am not sure how you see yourself in your dreams, but this particular dream is about the only time I ever *saw* myself in a dream. Usually when I dream it is me being me - like the dream is really happening in real time. I also dream in vivid colors, so the combination of these two components makes it difficult to know if my dreams are really happening, have happened or are going to happen. That gets very frustrating at times, especially as I get older.

I think I have always had a sense there is much more out there. Maybe I have been around for a really long time; maybe that is why I am not afraid of much; and maybe that is why I am able to communicate easily with people. Honestly, there isn't anyone I cannot start a conversation with, and I feel like I have known them forever. My Aunt May's psychic also made many predictions that to this day have come true: That I would help people; I would dance; and that I was worldly beyond my years. I still have the cassette tape the session was recorded on, but nothing to play it on. I would love to be able to listen to it again.

Having a sense there is something out there and experiencing it are two different things. A more recent experience (2011) was during a trip to San Antonio to see our niece get married. Of course the wedding was beautiful and of course the weather was great, and of course when you go to a new city you explore everything the city has to offer. You go to the downtown district, you check out the museums, and in this case you visit the historic River Walk area. This area was filled with restaurants, shops, churches, historic hotels, and the ever-popular River Walk. But, the scary part was when we visited the Alamo.

The day we visited the downtown area there was a festival, and I was intrigued by some booths that had men dressed in period clothes with authentic rifles and guns. I stopped and listened to them explain how they defended themselves, and about the simplicity of their gear and guns during the Civil War. Seemed like I already knew so much about them, but I was so caught up in their stories I lost track of time. My family had been waiting in line to enter the Alamo. When it was our turn to enter, Mark (my husband) was yelling at me to get over there so we could all go in together. As soon as we entered the main building I stopped as it was cooler in there than I had anticipated. I stood still and just looked around for a moment, looking at all the tourists peering into the dungeon-like rooms. I took a few more steps forward and stopped. I was actually kind of chilly. I thought to myself, *this is odd.* I took a few more steps and stopped dead in my tracks, I was standing smack dab in the middle of the room and then I froze. The tourists disappeared (well, not really) and I began to see soldiers in the building dressed in period uniforms fighting, ducking from gun fire, getting shot, falling down and some were even lying on the ground - dead. I heard voices and yelling, and chaos and commotion, and gunfire and I began to shake, tremble and cry uncontrollably. Right in the middle of this big room I was gasping for air, shaking like a leaf and sobbing like a baby. Mark turned around to see where I had gone only to see me panicking. He came over to me and asked what was wrong. I could not answer him because I was sobbing and gasping for air. I tried to tell him what I was seeing, but I could not utter a single word. All I could do was run for the exit. I pushed a few people out of the way, and I managed to get out of the building. I stopped on the sidewalk, which was still very close to the building and obviously still on the property grounds. After a few minutes I stopped shaking violently, but I could not stop gasping for air or crying. I paced and paced and told Mark when he found me that I was getting better, I would be okay, and to continue on exploring this historic place. I continued to pace for a few more minutes, still not feeling 100 percent right, so I bolted for the perimeter exit. I just could not be in there. I had to get the heck out of there as soon as I could. The people around me probably thought I was a lunatic or needed medication, or forgot to take my medication. As soon as I was outside of the historic grounds, instantly my breathing returned to normal and I stopped shaking.

I am not really sure what the people around me must have thought, and I really didn't care, but I am certain I gave them something to talk about. I waited outside for about 10 to 15 minutes and decided I would try again. I really did want to see the Alamo. I went back through the line and walked through the main doors like I did the first time and within moments of entering the building I had the same response: crying, sobbing, shaking and gasping. I ran out of the building and headed straight for the exit - I needed to get the heck off the grounds.

I slowly made my way to the main street and found a seat in the sun and sat there until everyone else finished touring the grounds. I was perfectly content to look at the Alamo from afar. Clearly, I was not supposed to be inside the building. Not really sure what to make of that ordeal, I had never seen so many men in period uniforms fighting and falling over, and I never want to see it again. Makes me wonder if one of the soldiers I saw was me, or was I a wife of a soldier and I was watching my husband get shot? I should have thought to look down and see what I was wearing. Did I have on military boots? Was I wearing an apron? Maybe I could have had a better understanding of what my role was as I was watching the action. Of course, my family joked about this the rest of the day, and this incident, like all the others, go into the bank of jokes and stupid things that Lorraine has done over the years. Someone has to provide the comic relief in the family and somehow that person is always me. It is always Lorraine who screws something up and then everyone talks about it forever.

So, it seems I have some abilities to tap into a deeper realm - without asking to go there - now, let me tell you about the time I did ask.

I was in 6th or 7th grade and a friend of mine was dabbling in witchcraft. I was intrigued by what she was doing so we would hold séances, or try to summon spirits with the Ouija board. I summoned more than I bargained for and was not a fan of the dark side that presented itself. Talk about evil, fear, hatred and pain. I promptly decided after I was asking the spirits to make things move and fall - and they did - that I did not want any part of that world. I never tried to summon anyone or anything ever again, now the spirits just find me whether I want them to or not.

To this day any feelings I have of things I sense when I see something paranormal or something that just isn't normal, I am not afraid, but actually welcome the experiences and find them to be rather peaceful.

At this point, you are probably thinking I am crazy and where exactly am I going with all this babble? Well, I am just trying to paint a picture of my childhood. One that was fun, happy, enjoyable and blessed. I got to do many things, go many places and I enjoyed every moment of it.

THREE

DANCE, PRANCE AND POSE

My mom never thought twice about enrolling me in something she knew I had an interest in, and joining the Jean Henderson Modeling School in the late 1960's was what I wanted to do. Not really sure why I wanted to model, but getting dressed up and parading around seemed like fun: little did I realize what modeling would teach me. It taught me poise, manners, proper posture and, yes, we used to walk with a book on the top of our head! I loved to model! It was actually a great complement to dancing when I look back on it.

Those that know me now know I have very short hair, but when I was young I had hair down to my lower back and beyond. I was tall and lean, and loved to ham it up, so modeling was a good fit for me. I also loved being in front of a camera. I had many opportunities while modeling to pose for print ads and walk the catwalk. I was even selected to be in the Sears catalog and I shot a Chevrolet car commercial.

Print ads were my least favorite because you had to sit still. It did not seem natural and it was not my style. The catwalk or runway, however, was a blast, because I got to dress up in the latest bell-bottoms and strut my stuff. What was there not to like?

Even though being selected to be in the Sears catalog was a big deal, it was still print work. Not sure which year I was in the catalog or if I even have a copy, but I do remember people could not wait to get it in the mail and look at all the latest trends. The catalog was almost as big as a phone book!

The car commercial, however, was my favorite. It was shot on some school grounds in Fort Lauderdale. My *mom* and *dad* drove up in their wooden paneled station wagon, which had white walled tires to pick up my *brother* and me. We ran down this grassy field from the school to the car carrying our books, which were strapped together with one of those giant rubber bands. We got in the car and drove off. Not sure how long the commercial aired and I could not even begin to tell you who my TV family was, in fact, I don't think I ever saw them again after that shoot.

I modeled for years. I enjoyed it and I guess it paid well. I never really knew how much money I made because I never asked: I just liked what I did. If I ever wanted to become a professional model then I needed to have a portfolio. A portfolio is to modeling what a resume is to corporate America. It is a compilation of photographs showcasing your best features. Once you had your portfolio you could then begin to audition for elite modeling agencies. I went through all the hoops to get my portfolio printed. I am pretty sure my parents spent a small fortune, but it was something I wanted to do. I remember going to a variety of auditions. Sometimes I got the jobs and sometimes I didn't. I remember being told my ears were not even (the right one is actually a little higher than the left) and I would never be a print model. *Really, uneven ears?* Nevertheless, I continued to work in South Florida for years, and at the same time I enrolled and began taking dance classes.

FOUR

DANCE LIKE NO ONE – OR EVERYONE – IS WATCHING

I actually started taking ballet classes at the age of three at the local community center. I do not really remember going to classes there, but around the age of six I do remember joining Ms. D'Avery Boca Raton Dance Academy. She was a beautiful, graceful and mild-mannered dancer/teacher/role model, which instilled in me the qualities of hard work and discipline. I loved taking dance classes. I loved to move freely and express how I felt through music. Dancing was a natural thing for me. It was something I enjoyed and something I did very well. I took traditional ballet classes, but I also took jazz, tap and eventually modern classes. I learned the Cecchetti method. This is a strict training method that focuses on the anatomy -

allowing the dancer to learn to dance by internalizing and expressing their emotions rather than by mimicking what the ballet mistress executed. Ultimately, you become the part you dance: You never just go through the motions. I attended ballet classes every single day after school from 3 p.m.-6 p.m. I took three different classes each day, and I worked my tail off. If we were practicing for a recital, we danced and rehearsed on the weekends as well and often for five to eight hours at a time. Perfection was needed, cohesion was needed, and you did it until you got it right! You did it until everyone got it right.

My biking accident could have put a damper on my rehearsing. But, I did not have a choice. I had to rehearse. So I learned from a very early age, there are NO EXCUSES, you did what was required of you and you did it with a smile.

Now I don't want you to think my childhood was all work and no play. I had my fair share of playground time, and I even attempted to learn how to surf, but I never played any kind of organized sports. I would have been good at them, but instead I chose to spend most of my after school hours at the dance studio in leotards, tights and pointe shoes (this might be the reason that today I like loose fitting clothes and shoes that flop around on my feet or no shoes at all).

Every dance studio in every city, in every state, likely performs "*The Nutcracker*" during the holidays and our dance studio was no different. We also rehearsed and performed everything from "*Giselle*" to "*All that Jazz*." When we rehearsed, we would wear leg warmers, cut up shirts, flowing pink skirts and headbands (think back to the late '70s and early '80s: think Jane Fonda and the movie "*Flash Dance*"). We may have looked ridiculous, but that is what a dancer wore, the sloppier and more tattered the clothing, the better, even the pointe shoes.

A pointe shoe is like a ballet slipper except with a hard box that your toes fit in to. It kind of feels like putting a square around a round peg, and they hurt! Our parents would spend $50-60 for one pair of pointe shoes. The shoes were so clean and shiny. But new shoes were not ready to dance in. Before you could dance in them, you had to scrape the bottoms so you didn't slip; smash the hard toe box in a doorframe so your toes weren't so cramped; and then you stood in water so they formed to your feet. It was a process: They had to be just right. Then maybe they were ready. Oops, I forgot we had to bend them in half - for what seemed like a gazillion times - to break in the arches. THEN they were ready. Sadly a pair of pointe shoes maybe lasted a few weeks. I never really knew how much money my parents invested in all my dancing clothes, shoes and tuition until I learned about budgeting and paying my own bills. Wow, the shoes, costumes, hairspray, makeup, gas to get to rehearsals, etc. It must have cost them a small fortune, but they must have believed in me, and I must have been good because I kept at it. At the age of 11, I auditioned for, and was accepted into, the Palm Beach Ballet Company (PBBC). This was a much bigger company and more well known in South Florida. It was also a 60-mile round trip drive from home. But that did not matter, my mom would pick me up from school, drive to the studio where I would take classes (sometimes until 8 p.m. or 9 p.m.), then drive home, help me with any homework and then we would repeat the next day. We did this for years!

In my early days with the PBBC, we performed at many venues such as parks, festivals and parades. We performed at the Burt Reynolds dinner theater and at the Poinsettia playhouse in Palm Beach. Each and every performance gave us more experience and more opportunities to perfect our own style and technique. At that time most of the dancing I did was ballet with the tutus, tights, pointe shoes and slicked back hair knotted in a tight bun.

Our performances consisted of bits and pieces from ballets, original works from our ballet mistress and sometimes-full acts from a ballet. My favorite ballet? Well, I liked them all. I liked the rigidity of "*Swan Lake,*" the precision of "*Don Quixote,*" the grace and flow of "*Giselle*" and the lightness of "*Coppelia.*" But, my favorite was the "*Nutcracker*" because we performed it every year. The story about a young girl who dreams of a nutcracker prince. There is a party scene, a fight scene, the land of sweets and the land of snow. And, of course, there is the dance of the sugar plum fairy. It was a magical performance for the holidays.

Along with our local performances, there were regional events. One of the more memorable events with the PBBC was an annual trip to perform in the SERBA (South East Regional Ballet Association) competition. Dance troupes from all over the southeast region would gather in some southern state and perform a piece they had been rehearsing for months. The year we attended, we performed "*Tarantella,*" an Italian folk ballet with tambourines and lots of jumping. I believe we came in third out of all the troupes that performed. We were good!

The bad thing about dance performances, like most other things you train for, is our recitals are over within a matter of seconds or minutes. All the months and/or years of hard work flash by in what seems to be a nanosecond. There are NO do over's; there are NO second chances. If a performer falls or messes up, they know deep down inside they gave it their all and did their best. Our ballet instructors expected nothing less than perfection. You kept trying until you figured out what was not right or how to make it better. There were never excuses; there was never "I'm tired." If you wanted to dance professionally, you did whatever it took to be perfect and nothing less!

Just like modeling, I absolutely loved being on stage; the lights, the audience, the scenery, all eyes and people watching you. It made me feel so large and strong, and powerful. If there is one thing I miss most now it would be being on stage. I took care of that when I started bodybuilding – which I will tell you all about in a later chapter.

Professional ballet studios often brought in famous dancers and guest teachers for us to learn from and work with. We all had hopes that maybe they would recognize our talent and whisk us away to New York or some other big city and ask us to join their company. Though that rarely (I mean never) happened, it could have and that is what we dreamt about.

The Miami Ballet Company was probably the best known company in South Florida during the 1970s and occasionally some of the PBBC dancers would get the opportunity to join their company for a master class or a performance. The Miami Ballet was such a big company that their shows and performances garnered giant names in the dance industry - Rudolph Nureyev, Maria Tallchief and Mikhail Baryshnikov. Wow, to be able to dance on the same stage with them - what an honor.

I remember I was once given that chance, and the ballet to be performed was *"Swan Lake."* I was so excited to be selected to be a part of the Corps de Ballet (these are not the principal dancers). Those selected to perform would not only take our usual dance classes and rehearse for our own shows; we would also travel to Miami once or twice a week to rehearse with their dance troupe. Honestly, I am not really sure how I graduated from high school when all I did was drive to and from rehearsals. Nonetheless, I had the opportunity to dance in the corps with the Miami Ballet Company and to share the stage with Rudolph Nureyev. Yes, Rudolph Nureyev!!!

The star of the show never arrived until a day or two before the actual performance and when they did arrive we would sit in the theater seats and watch them rehearse. Rudolph Nureyev was amazing! His jumps were so high – it looked like he was flying and he executed his pirouettes with grace and speed. I could barely count how many turns he did because he was spinning so fast. Two days before the performance we obviously had to rehearse with him onstage and to see him up close was even more amazing. Honestly, I consider a dancer to be better conditioned than any other athlete. A dancer must have the speed of a sprinter, the precision of a golfer, the grace of an ice skater, the power and strength of a football player and the endurance of a marathoner. Unlike most athletes a dancer also had to perform with a smile at all times.

I actually did get to meet Rudolph Nureyev, shake his hand and take pictures with him, and I have his autograph somewhere. He signed my ballet program and the back of a picture. Regardless, I shared the stage with one of the most famous dancers in history. That, my friend, looks great on any resume!

During the summer months, we didn't have as many performances, which gave dancers a chance to spend a month or two in summer workshops often with some professional dance company. Since my family was from Pittsburgh, I enrolled with the Pittsburgh Ballet Theatre during the months of June and July. My mom and I would leave at the end of the school year, fly to Pittsburgh, stay with my aunt and uncle, and take the bus into the city to the well-known dance theater where I took classes five times/week. The dance studios of a professional company were gigantic, complete with a piano, mirrors and boxes of rosin. Attending summer workshops such as these earned you the opportunity to audition for an apprenticeship with the company if they thought you were good enough to become part of their professional troupe. An apprenticeship was the next step in becoming a professional dancer, which is every girl's dream. Well, it was my dream. How exciting for a young ballerina to earn that chance. It was like making the Olympics, or earning an Oscar. It was the big time!

You see, there were never any excuses allowed. Your dance instructors did not care that you had a blister on every toe, and that most of the time they were bleeding; they did not care if you had a strained muscle; or if you had cramps, or if you were sick. They did not care if you went out and partied the night before. It did not matter! They took and accepted NO EXCUSES. You showed up for class and did what you were told, and you did it until you got it right. I guess all the years of being pushed to, and beyond my limits, made me the strong-willed person I am today. I was never going to give in. I was never going to disappoint my teachers, my fellow dancers or my parents. I was never going to give any performance anything less than 210 percent. Because the culmination of being on stage and giving the best performance you ever gave made all those long hours of rehearsing, all those bloody toes, lost toenails, strained and pulled muscles, worth it. The audience's applause because they truly liked what you did - not because the performance was over- was the most gratifying experience ever. Trust me when I say you can tell the difference between applause because you are finished, and applause because you did a great job!

But dancing is not all about taking classes, rehearsing, make-up, costumes and being on stage. There is another aspect of the dance world that is even more damaging than the aches and pains of hours and hours of jumping, leaping and turning; it is the desire to be as thin as possible. You never want to hear your partner say, "Yo fat-ass, how many burgers did you eat last night?" You had to be light on your feet and light as a feather. This was a part of the dance world that was ugly and secretive, and yet it was something that was so common that no one ever thought there was anything wrong with the behavior.

I do not recall any girls who had eating issues back when I was dancing in Boca, but I do recall there were many girls in the PBBC who had severe eating disorders; both anorexics and bulimics. Anorexics don't eat at all or just nibble on their food. Bulimics eat to excess and then purge (vomit) all the food they ate. Both are horrid ways to live and both have many life-long emotional and psychological consequences. I will always remember one gal who got so thin she looked like a toothpick with a giant bobble head. She was an anorexic and wanted nothing more than to be a professional dancer. She would do whatever it took to get there; she got so thin that most of her hair fell out. We were all worried about her and knew something was seriously wrong. I think she was asked to take a leave of absence until she gained some weight and some strength.

She was not the only one with issues. Honestly, we all ate like crap. Those who starved themselves and survived on 500 calories a day had little strength. They always looked gaunt and were usually pale white. Those who did eat sometimes gorged and then vomited everything they ate. Some of us drank, partied and ate fast food; some of us smoked and some used illegal drugs to give us the energy needed since we were not getting it from nutritious food. I did not know then much about fueling my fire (metabolism), or how food affected my performance, or that there were 'good' and 'bad' foods. Remember, this was long before I knew a lick about nutrition. What I did know was it takes a lot of energy to rehearse for hours on end, thus food should have been our friend not our foe!

People typically eat when they are hungry. Sometimes, though, they eat when they are tired, stressed, bored, angry or anxious. Food can be comforting to some, and it is something you can control. Too often then not, it is used as a reward. People forget the real purpose of food, which is to supply the body with energy; it cannot and should not be used to fill a void.

What I have never been able to understand is one's ability to get past the hunger signals. When my belly growls, I listen and I eat. I never understood how some dancers could just act like it wasn't a big deal. I actually think I weighed a little more then than I do now. I ate whatever I wanted. Heck, I was going to dance and practice for hours.

I clearly remember there was a smoothie place near one of the dance studios where I would get a peanut butter smoothie after class. Oh, how I looked forward to this giant cup filled with vanilla ice cream, peanut butter and a banana. There was also a 7-11 across the street where I would often get a giant bag of flaming hot Fritos and eat the entire bag on my way home. Remember, I often didn't have time for dinner as I went right from school to the dance studio and was there for hours and hours on end. When I turned 16 and got my driver's license I drove myself to and from dance class. I am sure this was a huge relief on my mom, but it made it more difficult for me, as I was not able to eat or do my homework while I drove.

I had a few close dance friends who I would sometimes stay with on Friday nights, since I had to be back at the dance studio early Saturday mornings. We had a blast together. We did things we should not have done. I remember smoking cigarettes and drinking alcohol. We would often get dressed up and go to the bars and dance till the wee hours of the morning. Sometimes we would order pizzas or burgers, and I would overeat. I will admit I did try the bulimic thing because I felt guilty for shoveling all that food into my body. I did not like the fullness and really always thought about my dance partner saying, "Yo fat-ass, what did you eat last night?" I have never verbalized that to anyone or written that anywhere. No one knows I did it or tried it. Well, maybe they did and never said anything or maybe I just disguised it too well. Eating disorders are one of those issues that seem to surface and then hide only to come back and rear its ugly head over and over again! As I write this I realize that dancers are one messed up group of girls.

To this day I maintain friendships with some of my dancing friends. There are some I cannot locate and some I don't want to locate. But, we had our share of fun and for that I will be forever grateful.

Your best chances at becoming a ballerina are really only possible when you are young, before your body matures. Much like a gymnast, the time to shine is before your menstrual cycle begins, before you grow boobs and a butt. Sure, there are exceptions but generally this was the way it was. So, you did everything in your power to be the very best you could be because you only had a few years at making the 'big time'.

The art of dance instills in you a sense of drive, dedication, determination, perfection and relentless practice to getting it right. To this day, I still follow and adhere to the same approach. I set my mind on a goal and dedicate my time, training and eating to helping myself achieve said goal. I strive for perfection and I am determined to try over, and over, and over, until I get it right. It is good or bad, right or wrong, black or white, which are qualities that can be very maddening and frustrating. But, I never ever wanted to say, "Well, I wish I had tried harder!" I wanted to say, "I gave it everything I had and I did my best."

FIVE

SCHOOL TIME, DEAR OLD GOLDEN RULE TIME

As you have read, I spent most of my 'tween and teenage years in a dance studio. Yes, I went to school, and, no, I did not like it. Who in the heck needs to know how to dissect a frog or find the coefficient of 42 in order to dance on stage? I really took zero interest in school. I attended Boca Raton Academy. It was a smaller private school, and I think there were somewhere around 75 students in my grade. I had a few close friends, and I got along with everyone, but, I did not play any sports, and I was not part of any clubs, so my time with my classmates was just during school hours. The teachers were fair and the homework was boring...blah, blah, blah. At the time I had no intention in going to college, so I did not care about my GPA. I just really wanted to dance!

High school was - as it is for most - a rebellious time or a time to test the limits. No, I did not get thrown in jail. No, I did not get busted for drugs and I did not get voted as class clown, but I did have fun. I never skipped classes, smart mouthed my teachers or was disrespectful in any way, and I actually got fairly decent grades.

During my senior year, I did have a working internship at IBM that required 25 hours of my time (like I didn't have enough on my plate). There were a few of us who did go out on the weekends to the local clubs and dance or drink (water!). KC and the Sunshine Band used to play all the time at the Holiday Inn on Glades Road. It was always fun to dance in a club vs. dance in a studio. It felt really good to enjoy the music and move freely without worrying about whether your toes were pointed or your kicks were high enough. Outside of the few friends I had at school, most of the people I hung out with were my dancing friends and I remember I always dated older guys: guys that had *big-boy* jobs and cars, and money.

There are only two class functions I remember attending; Grad Nite and our senior cruise.

For Grad Nite we traveled by Greyhound bus to Orlando only to spend one full day there. My boyfriend at the time went with me. Why he would want to spend time with all of my high school classmates I have no clue. But, I remember having a great time.

For our senior trip, we took a three-day cruise to the Bahamas. My boyfriend also joined me for this event, and again we had a great time. The weather was perfect; the islands spectacular; and the food and drinks plentiful.

During my senior year I did enroll in some college classes at Palm Beach Junior College (PBJC) - I only had a few high school credit hours to fulfill so it was required that I attend a higher learning institute. Whatever! I took some accounting classes, which helped with my internship position at IBM, and I believe I took some type of English class. All I remember is that I had papers to write and midterms to take. If that was what college was all about, I did not want any part of it.

I also remember during my senior year I was sick a lot - lots of belly issues. Not really sure what they were all about, but I remember always being tired and sore, and not feeling 100 percent. However, this never stopped me from dancing, going out or going to the beach. Remember I had a NO EXCUSES attitude: Grin and bear it and move along with your day.

SIX

TIME TO JAZZ IT UP A BIT

As I mentioned before, my goal was to be accepted into a major ballet company as an apprentice, so as I approached my junior and senior years of high school, I began to audition for professional ballet companies. I wanted nothing more than to be a principal dancer, which means dancing solo. I wanted to stand out - be center stage - so everyone was watching just me! I thrived on the pressure. I enjoyed the challenge of knowing I had to get it just right. I never realized at the time there was a name for my obsession; Obsessive Compulsive Disorder (OCD). A person with true OCD would put the acronym in the right order, so it would be CDO *(hahahaha)*. Honestly, I was not always so obsessed with every component of my life. I did not need to have the clothes in my closet hanging in color-order and I did not need to have my record albums in alphabetical order. But I did have to have my dance routines perfected. I did have to wear my special leotard or leg warmers. I did have my rituals before a performance. So I guess in some respects I did have some order issues.

I remember auditioning for three ballet companies, but waiting for the acceptance or rejection letter was always the hardest part. There were usually many dancers trying out for a select few spots and you remember how great they were and wonder, *"Was I good enough? Did I do enough? Did I remember to smile?"* And then you think, *"Yes, yes I did. I gave it my all,"* this is what I was working toward. When the envelope/s finally arrived, you think, *"My future is in this envelope."* It is like a high school graduate who is holding their potential college acceptance letter. They are frozen; they can't open it; they just stand there and stare at it; maybe let it sit for a few days till they get the nerve to open it. Who am I kidding? No one ever does that. They usually rip that baby open as soon as it arrives. Well, I did get my letters, and I did open them as quickly as I could only to learn I was accepted into all three apprentice programs at the Milwaukee Ballet, Houston Ballet and the Pittsburgh Ballet Theatre. How fortunate and lucky was I? All my years of hard work, aches, sprains and pulled muscles paid off. I was thrilled beyond belief, yet so unsure of what to do.

As I began to explore my options I learned ballerinas did not make much money. Dancing professionally had never been about the money; it was always about the love, the drive and the passion. But one begins to think, I will have to pay for an apartment, food, transportation, pointe shoes and other ballet gear. No wonder all ballerinas look tattered and torn. They cannot afford anything! And, what if I wanted to come home for the holidays - even a long weekend - how would I pay for that? I knew the long and hard hours of classes and practice did not quite add up to the pay. And there would not have been any extra time to get a part-time job. *Hmm, now what?* Not follow my dream? No way! I was going to dance no matter what or where.

Earlier I mentioned that even though ballet was my first passion I also took jazz, tap and modern classes. No matter what type of dance I ended up doing I knew I would enjoy it. Each type of dance has its own style and freedom of expression. Modern dance was not my cup of tea! I am not an Alvin Alley flop around type of dancer. Tap dancing was fun, but again, not really my style and how many professional tap dancers can one name? Really, think about it. Can you even name one? Well, let me help you out: there was

Ginger Rodgers, Fred Astaire and Gregory Hines. I am sure there are plenty of others, but these three were amazing. Jazz, however, I really enjoyed. It was more my style. It was upbeat, fast, spunky and sassy. There was more creative freedom to add your own style and flair, and the costumes were much more exciting! But, the style of jazz we learned and performed at the ballet studios was more subdued and very different than what I ultimately ended up doing.

As I mentioned before, dancers often took master classes with other dance companies. This was a way to get more practice and exposure. I took many master ballet classes, but most of the master jazz classes I took were at a studio in Fort Lauderdale with dance mistress Magda Aunon. The classes there were geared more toward the flirty jazz style. More showgirl style, if you will. I also, on occasion, joined my friend from PBBC and took a jazz class with a company (also in Fort Lauderdale) called Jean Ann Ryan (JAR) Productions. These classes were hard-core: showgirl-style with lots of high kicks, precision and flare. I loved all the classes I took; whether my belly felt good or not, I loved the way dancing made me feel.

I took these master classes at the same time I was auditioning for professional ballet companies. Up until this point there was nothing in my world except school, dancing, rehearsing, performing and the occasional homework. Since I spent so many hours dancing, I often worked through aches and pains, and blisters and sprains, and strains. NO EXCUSES. I did what was asked of me.

I had a smaller shape; I was kind of lanky and kind of looked like a box or a boy. I never had that hourglass shape. My weight fluctuated between 95 and 105. I was never concerned if it dipped too low: I would just eat a few bags of Fritos and drink giant smoothies, and I would be right back to fightin' weight. In general, I thought my overall health was OK. My belly ached on occasion. Oh, who was I kidding? It ached a lot and almost every day some foods would bother it and some foods would not. I just attributed it to my choices and nothing more. I did smoke on occasion, and I did drink - all the things dancers are not supposed to do. So, if I had any pains unrelated to dancing, I just worked through them and went about striving for my goal to be center-stage.

I had a few big decisions ahead of me: Do I accept an apprenticeship position with a ballet company or do I stay closer to home and audition for a Vegas style revue on one of the local cruise lines? These were two totally different options and styles of dancing. I had not really considered being a showgirl. I wanted to be a ballerina, but being a showgirl seemed like it might be a ton of fun. The more I learned about it, I found out I would get to travel and I would be home on the weekends. This could work. The dance routines for a Vegas-style showgirl revue were less intense. I did not say they were easier or there weren't lots of rehearsals; it was just that the dance numbers were not as rigid. To be a showgirl one has to have a rockin' hot body, have high kicks and be able to swish, flirt and flaunt their stuff. And, if you think back to my modeling days, swishing, flirting and flaunting my stuff was a piece of cake.

The more I asked around, I found out the Norwegian Cruise Line (NCL) was going to be holding auditions for their fall/winter contracts. I learned that even though the pay was not great, it paid more than what I would get as an apprentice with a ballet company, and I did not have to pay for room and board. Plus I would be in port every weekend, so I could go home if I needed something or wanted to see my folks. Basically, I would get paid to travel! I would get paid to relax on the beach and swim in the ocean. I thought, what the heck, let's go to this audition and see what happens. I had been taking classes there anyway, they knew me and my abilities so what is the worst that could happen? They didn't pick me, and I would go back to Plan A and pick a ballet company.

The day came in mid-April for me to audition for JAR Productions. I will admit, I was nervous. I arrived at the dance studio in Fort Lauderdale, signed in and got my nametag. Then I did what all dancers do - I sized up my competition while waiting, warming up and making small chat with the other dancers. When the production team is ready to begin the audition, they introduce themselves, tell everyone to be themselves and do their best. The audition begins by breaking down the dance piece that everyone is going to be performing. The production team goes through the piece a few times and everyone tries like hell to remember it. Then it's your turn to perform it. They want to see how fast, and how quickly, the dancers move. They cue the music and everyone gets a few attempts to go through the piece and then everyone is asked to perform the piece as a group. The group goes through the piece a few times while the production team is sizing everyone over. Then each dancer is asked to perform the piece individually. Just you - all eyes on you. That is when you sell yourself. When you show them what you can do. I loved this part!

After all the dancers have performed the piece, they are asked to do some individual moves such as pirouettes, jumps and some partnering work. They want to look at everyone's technique, training, style, how they move and how precise they are. This is where my years of ballet came into play. I am thinking to myself, "*I got this.*" I have always picked up things quickly: Show me once and I will do it.

I felt the audition went really well. I was in a room with 15-20 other dancers, all vying for a few select spots on the NCL cruise line. I did know a few of the people there as we have danced together at various times over the last 12 years. We all do our thing, the production team thanks you for attending and says... "We will be in touch." What the heck does that mean? Does that mean I will get a call tomorrow? In a week? What? When? I never have been a patient person, so this waiting business was just not cool!

For the next few days, I sat on pins and needles waiting for my future to be decided. Am I going to become a showgirl or a ballerina? Either way it was OK. I would be dancing and that is what mattered most. A few days later, Jean Ann Ryan's assistant called to tell me I had been selected to become part of the NCL cast and if I accepted, my contract would begin in September. WOO-HOO! I don't think I have ever jumped that high. How cool is this? I am going to be a showgirl on a cruise ship. I called all my friends and told them the great news. Remember this is 1982; there wasn't Facebook or Twitter so that one could post to the world the current events of their life as they unfolded. Wow, my future was decided for me. It was definitely not how I thought things were going to turn out. I did call the ballet companies who had offered me apprenticeship programs and declined their offers. That was scary because what if something happened and the cruise contract fell through? Then what would I do? But, if this was the path I was meant to be on it would all work out.

Regardless, I had to finish my senior year, and then I would have time to enjoy summer before my contract began. I don't know if I was stressing because of finals, working at IBM in addition to taking classes at PBJC, the thoughts of leaving home, the pressure of being on my own, or what. But, my belly started hurting again. Then there was a gradual feeling of lethargy that set in. I found myself sleeping more; I always felt like I was running a fever. My appetite waned and I was losing weight. I didn't want to go out, I just wanted to lay on the couch. This really had been going on for months, but I just chalked it up to all that was going on. I was not sure who this person was I had turned into. It certainly was not me! But I plugged along as I always did. NO EXCUSES - push through - be strong and that is what I did. I made sure I focused on my school finals and I continued my dance classes. But something was not physically right and I just couldn't put my finger on it.

SEVEN

WHERE THE STORY BEGINS

About a month after auditioning for Jean Ann and shortly after my high school graduation I got a call from JAR Productions. They told me a cast member was not going to be fulfilling her contract and they needed someone to fill her place immediately. Oh my gosh! I was beyond excited. I don't think I have screamed so loudly, ran around so fast or jumped so high. It is here: The beginning of my professional dancing career. They asked if I was available. Of course I was! School was out; I was free as a bird!

Joann (the assistant manager) said the position would start in June. Holy Ba-Geez! So soon? Next month, actually. Of course I said, "Yes!" Instead of having months to get ready, I only had about three weeks. My mom and I began by shopping for a steamer trunk. The cast I was joining split their time between two cruise ships, which meant I would be traveling throughout the week ultimately living out of a suitcase. But really, that was OK. All I needed was a bathing suit, some flip flops and a few outfits, right?!? Mom and I started shopping. We bought bathing suits, fancy dresses for the Captain's dinner, evening clothes, play clothes, shoes, toiletries, bags, makeup - we bought it all!

We had a lot of fun shopping and getting my things organized, but because I spent so much time with my mom it was hard for me to disguise the aches and pains, and frequent bathroom trips I was experiencing. And like me, my mom was no dummy. She knew something was up. She often asked what was wrong, and, of course, I always said nothing, because NOTHING was going to stop me from beginning my dancing career.

The pains I had been having were getting much worse and more intense much like someone was taking a steak knife and digging it all around my gut. When I say gut I am referring to the area below my belly button and between my hipbones. My stomach was fine!

When a pain came on I would leave the room as quickly as possible. The pain was often so severe it would bring me to my knees and I would have to curl up into the fetal position until it passed. Sometimes the pain would last a few seconds and sometimes a few minutes. I tried not to let any whimpers out. *Me cry?* That is so not like me and, quite frankly, very funny when I think about it.

I couldn't find any rhyme or reason to the timing of the pain. What the heck was going on with me? Now, don't get me wrong, I am certainly familiar with pain. Remember, I danced with bloody toes, strained and pulled muscles, and I did it with a smile, so pain was nothing new to me. But, this pain was so different. It made the tired, sore or pulled muscles seem like a paper cut.

I had also started using the bathroom on a very frequent basis. Not to get graphic, but these were not your traditional bathroom visits; these required urgency and the formation of things changed quite a bit, if you know what I mean. Not to mention, I could race to the bathroom, think I was finished, get up, walk out the bathroom door, only to turn right around and run back in and sit back down. And this, mind you, might happen two, three or four times!

In addition, I did feel like I had a fever and, yes, I was tired, but it was hot in Florida and I danced all the time. I didn't think twice about it until I started getting these strange red, raised, hot-to-the-touch bumps on my shins; kind of like gi-nor-mous zits. Yes, that is gross, but that is what they looked liked. I am talking they were the size of quarters or bigger. There were quite a few of these raised red spots, but somehow I was able to keep them hidden with leg warmers. I remember when I stood up and the blood rushed down my legs, the spots throbbed. Sitting with my legs propped up was a good thing. Actually cool compresses felt better, but that was kind of hard to disguise. Along with my gut aches and pains, the frequent trips to the bathroom, my decreased desire to eat or go out with my friends was a cause for concern and a red flag that something was wrong.

By the time we finished buying all the items I thought I was going to need for my new job, my mom could tell I was in serious pain. When I tried on clothes she could tell I was wasting away. She finally put two and two together, and realized I was always in the bathroom; I had zero desire to go to the beach or out with my friends; and I was very pale and gaunt looking. One day Mom asked to take my temperature - 104 degrees. Hmm, no wonder why I felt so hot and tired, and crabby. Every day for the next few days we took my temp and it did not go down. Then one day she forced me to take off the leg warmers and she saw these awful large bumps that looked like they were ready to explode. Well at that point, as any good mom would do, she called my doctor to schedule an appointment for me to get an evaluation. I really did not want to go, but I was so tired and so worn down, and so over trying to put on a happy face, I went. If I did not figure this out, there was NOT going to be a cruise ship contract. The sooner we knew what was going on, the better.

My doctor was my neighbor, a general practitioner. I explained all the symptoms I had been experiencing over the last few weeks or maybe even months. I showed him the bumps on my legs and I explained in detail the pain I had throughout my body. He took blood and ran some lab tests. I don't know what he was looking for and I don't remember if he ever told me the results. Even if he had I would not have known what the heck he was talking about. He ordered X-rays and suggested I see a gastroenterologist. A what? Can't you just give me a pill Doc? I got a cruise ship to catch! Oh no, this was not going to be that simple. Apparently, there was much more to this than I ever imagined.

EIGHT

NOW THE STORY REALLY BEGINS

I guess I do not remember, or I have blocked out the events of the following weeks. It seems there were doctor appointments after doctor appointments after doctor appointments. I met with a new doctor, this gastro-whatever. Nice guy, short guy, very sympathetic. We talked about all my issues and experiences over the last few months. He reviewed my lab work and then ordered more. Good thing needles did not bother me, as I felt nothing short of a pincushion with all this testing. I was also scheduled for something called an endoscopy and a colonoscopy. *What in the sam heck are those!?!* I read the informational pamphlet and cried. Oh my, this was not going to be any fun!

But the sooner we got this over with I could move along with my life. Little did I know?

I can clearly remember the preparation for these tests. The first test I had was an endoscopy. For this particular procedure one has to take some oral medications the day before, then on the day of the test they can have nothing to eat or drink (no biggie, at this point I was not eating or drinking much anyway). Once at the hospital and admitted, one is given a beautiful gown, then wheeled to the waiting area. Once there, one is handed a gallon-sized jug with something called barium. Barium was a flavored (like that made it all better) thick milky liquid that one was instructed to drink, because if they did not finish the entire jug the test could not be performed. The staff informed me my test was scheduled in one hour, so I better get started drinking. Really lady, my body was rejecting water, how can you expect me to drink this thick crap. Well, it was flavored! That made it all better! I tried my best to choke down this stuff so I could get this test over with. I succeeded just in time and as my reward I was wheeled into a sterile and cold testing room. There were cameras, TVs, monitors, tubes, tanks; oh I did not like the looks of this. Now don't get me wrong, the staff was very kind and helpful, but really this was over the top. I remember after I was positioned on the exam table, I was given something else to take that reminded me of Pop-Rocks - you know, the candy that exploded in your mouth. Well, these were not Pop Rocks; these were some kind of salts that I had to swallow. OK, I could do that, BUT I was then instructed NOT to burp. Now *that* I didn't know if I could do: You see, the salts expanded the GI tract so the docs could see what was going on, if you burped you *deflated* and the cameras and images the docs were taking were not as good, and the test might not be valid. This was going to be hard.

I had consumed my gallon of yummy thick liquid. I was half dressed in a hospital gown; I was cold; and I had to go to the bathroom. I swallowed the Pop Rocks and tried not to burp. Then, as I lay on this hard examining table, they positioned cameras over me. Seriously, I can do many things: Grande jete's, triple pirouettes, even fouettes, but this I was having trouble doing. Of course, I had to. NO EXCUSES. Just get this over with – let the staff do what they have to do so I could burp, fart and go to the bathroom. In reality, the test likely didn't last for more than a few minutes. I was asked to turn onto my right side, my left side, my back, hold still, don't breathe. *Come on people, you ever been on the receiving side of this test?* It ain't easy! But, I did what I was told. Finally I was allowed to sit up and let me tell you what - I let out a burp that even surprised me. But, I felt better and I am SURE I was not the first person to do that. Test one finished; now onto the colonoscopy.

Well, if the first test didn't humble me, the colonoscopy certainly did. *Seriously, I am a 17-year-old female; I have things I do not want you looking at.* This procedure was very different from the first one. I had to have an IV hooked up so they could give me some sleepy drops. Again, I am wheeled off into a cold and sterile room with cameras, tanks, hoses and other assorted "I don't know what's." The nurses did a fine job of explaining what would happen, but all I heard was, "Blah blah blah, and then you will wake up..." Whatever people: let's get going. Finally a familiar face enters the room - my doctor. I have only known this man for a few weeks and now here I lie on my side with my hospital gown draped around my bum and he is going to ... Oh, hell. Everyone knows how these tests go!

Well, back in the early days, they did things a little differently. You were asleep during the procedure, but you were awake at the same time. They told you what they were doing as they did it. They told you when they were adding air and when they were advancing the scope. Really, did this scope really belong so far up in my colon? Isn't this the exit only area! I felt the scope and I winced, I felt it advance and I winced some more. I felt the air and my belly distend.

I felt like I wanted to hide under a rock. When the docs decided they had seen enough they began to retract the tube and the air. They try to retract as much air as they put in, but there is always some residual air, so needless to say, you farted a lot the rest of the day. And the sleepy drops they gave you took forever to wear off. Well, at least they did with me. "Miss Stellute, can you hear me? Miss Stellute, can you open your eyes? Miss Stellute, can you...?" *LEAVE ME ALONE, you know what you just did to me and now you want me to spring out of this "comfortable" bed - put my pants on and go home? I can't even focus let alone sit up and move - please go away!*

Eventually, the sleepy drops wore off and I was able to coherently put together two words that made sense. I got dressed, and thought I was going to get to go home, but instead I had a one-way ticket to a hospital bed. As if the humility of all the testing was not bad enough, I had to be admitted because all my results and lab work were so out of whack.

I was devastated. Here I am ready to begin my dancing career - something I have worked toward my entire life - and instead I got admitted to the hospital. What if I lost my contract? What if they replaced me with another dancer? I declined my ballet internships to take this job. I likely couldn't call the ballet companies back with my tail between my legs and ask if a spot is still open. What was I going to do??? *I'm so afraid. I don't want this stress. Why now?*

Over the course of the next few days the staff, and nurses and doctors, poked and prodded and force-fed me food I did not like and would not eat. Well guess what – if you don't eat it you don't go home. Because if you don't eat, you don't poop and I had to have a bowel movement before they would release me. So there I lay, I am still sick and miserable, but getting better. I am still tired, but regaining some strength likely because I was hooked up to IV's and taking other oral medications. First line therapy in the early 1980s was steroids, so I was being pumped full of Prednisone, which actually made me kind of hungry, but it still hurt to eat.

I am glad my mom was there by my side because all I remember is the doctor telling me I had something called Crohn's disease. *HUH? What in the hell was that? Does it go away? Am I contagious? Can I still have children?* Again, this is 1982, not a lot of people had heard of this disease. Now don't get me wrong, I liked being first with a lot of things, but I did not need to be first with a disease. First in line for concert tickets, first in line to get your driver's license, first in line to ride the amusement park rides - that is OK, but first to be diagnosed with a disease no one knows much about. No thanks! I'll pass! Why pick me?

I do not want this role! I do not want to play this part. I am a NO EXCUSES kind of gal, but really, not now!" Cruise ships awaited me. There was fun to be had; I did not have time for this.

Over the course of my hospital stay the nurses and doctors explained the disease in medical words and terms I did not really understand – again, glad my mom was there because all I heard was "blah blah blah." I needed to stay on the steroids and I needed bed rest. And really, what the heck are steroids? The doctors prescribed many pills for me take that had very specific instructions and they explained the side effects. They gave me lots of reading materials. *Seriously, did you people just meet me, I don't read!* I don't like novels or textbooks; magazines are OK because of the pictures, but this boring technical, medical stuff, keep it! I just wanted the meds so I can get better and go home.

I will briefly describe the disease, but for full information about signs, symptoms, treatments, nutritional information and resources, refer to Chapter 36.

Crohn's disease is a chronic inflammatory condition of the gastrointestinal tract that belongs with a group of conditions known as inflammatory bowel disease (IBD).

Some of the symptoms include; diarrhea, urgency, cramps, bloating, fever, loss of appetite, weight loss, fatigue, and loss of menstrual cycle. Yup, I was quite familiar with each one of those. To date, about the only symptoms listed that I had not experienced were the night sweats, rectal bleeding, vision changes and arthritis. Oh, something to look forward to!

Since Crohn's is a chronic condition, I was told there would be times when I would be in remission, and there would be times when the Crohn's would flare, but it would never go away. Current treatment options were medicine, surgery and diet.

So there it is in a nutshell - Crohn's, the condensed version. As I continued to learn more about the disease I found out I might experience fissures (or tears) in the lining of the GI tract, which could cause pain and bleeding. Other fun tidbits I learned was that the disease was not well understood and it was thought that diet and stress may play a role. If diet and stress were culprits that would make sense as I did eat poorly. I would often drink and I did eat bags of chips at one time. I did stress about my career and dancing. Huh! Coincidence?

I also read that Crohn's cells attack themselves and an inflammatory response occurs hence the fever, and diarrhea, and potential arthritis. The body is trying to rid itself of something it thinks should not be there. Oh brother, this is why I hate reading stuff, now I have learned way more than I want to, and this was only one pamphlet. Remember no WebMD or Wikipedia back in 1982!!! Now I know of the multitude of things that can go wrong (symptom-wise), how do I fix this so I can get better? I want to learn about how I can make it go away – or go into remission.

As mentioned, first-line therapy in the mid-'80s was steroids. Steroids work by reducing or suppressing the immune system, thus allowing the system to not attack itself. Prednisone is one of those drugs and that is what they were giving me. Great, this drug sounded like it can do the trick. Sign me up! To not have any pain, to not run a constant fever, to not feel tired, that would be wonderful. So I began to read how these steroids work, then I continued reading to learn of all the possible side effects; increased pressure in the eye, swelling of the limbs, mood swings, increased blood pressure, weight gain, moon face, loss of calcium from the bone, dry mouth, thin skin, easy bruising and sore throat. These were the most common side effects, was taking this drug worth it or do I suffer? Which was going to be the lesser of the two evils?

Seems I did not have a choice, my doctor was quick to get me started on the IV prednisone cocktail so the inflammation would be reduced. After four or five days of treatments, I felt like a new person. My labs were back to normal and my belly did not hurt. This was fabulous. As much as I like being waited on, I really just wanted to sleep in my own waterbed, see my friends and maybe even go out dancing, for fun of course. Upon discharge I was instructed to take 100 mg of steroids daily for three weeks and then return for a follow-up appointment. Little did I know at the time what a huge dose of prednisone that was? I truly had no idea how this drug was going to affect me and little did I realize how it would affect me in 20, 30 or even 40 years from now. What I did, was do what I was told and I felt like a new person. I had energy, my muscles and joints did not hurt, my fever went away, the unbearable pain in my gut went away and my 9,000 trips to the bathroom decreased by half. *WOW, YIPPEE, HOORAY! This is great! I'm back!*

I was released to go home, I got settled in and got my medications and then reality kicked in: All the side effects of steroids I read about started to rear their ugly heads. The worst was the moon face: I looked like a chipmunk with acorns stuffed in its cheeks. I started growing this peach fuzz all over my face and arms, and my mood changed like the wind. I did start getting an appetite, but I really was not sure what to eat and the doctors just told me to eat what sounded good. I do remember one of the foods agreed with me was tuna and noodles. There was no way I could tolerate much. No vegetables, no fruits, no meats, dairy was questionable and the thought of fast food or fried food or Fritos made me cringe. Not sure how low my weight got, something tells me upper '80s. What I did know was when I found a food that agreed with me, I ate it. I quickly began to associate food as a means to an end. Food became nothing more for me than sustenance. I didn't eat because I liked to, or wanted to, or enjoyed it. I ate because I had to.

I spent most of July and August at home, bumming around, visiting my friends, going to the beach, hanging out and getting healthy. I did speak with Joann and Jean Ann who were extremely concerned, sympathetic and understanding, and they were kind enough to delay my contract until the fall. That was such an amazing relief to know I wasn't going to lose my contract. I could finally really relax.

Three weeks went by and we returned to the doctors for my follow up visit and lab work. At this point I was feeling pretty good. I had little to no gut pain, no joint pain, no fever and the giant red blisters on my shins had almost disappeared. Well I take that back, there was one rather large blister that did come to a head and burst. And to this day I have a scar about the size of a quarter where it left its mark. The doc was pleased with my progress and at this point he gave me a very detailed description of how I was to take the prednisone and how I was to (eventually) wean myself off of it. *Holy Ba-Gees? This was going to take up to nine months. What the heck?! How can I dance looking like a chipmunk?* Apparently you can experience severe withdrawal symptoms if you stop too quickly. Each week I could decrease my dosage by 5mg. And if, or when, I experienced any new pains I was to call him immediately. "Yeah, Yeah, Yeah, Doc, whatever, I will take my pills like I am told."

So, life went back to normal. I went out with my friends and I had the energy to start taking some dance classes again. This was actually the time I should have been cruising on the high seas, but instead I am stuck here in Boca. Well, let's just enjoy what was left of summer.

Life carried on until I got a surprise call on a random Friday in September. Apparently a cast member from the NCL Sunward left the show and JAR needed someone to replace her immediately and was I able to be on board by Tuesday. WTH! I had a good portion of my clothes ready from my previous preparations, but I was not anywhere ready to pack it all up and head out in a mere three days. Well I never moved so fast in my life, Mom and Dad, and I scrambled around to get my belongings packed and ready to go.

NINE

GOTTA GET, GOTTA GET, GOTTA GET YOUR SEALEGS

After 17 years, the time has finally come for me to begin my professional dancing career. There was nothing holding me back now. I remember arriving at the port of Miami and was totally overwhelmed by all the ships that were in port: all the people, tourists, luggage and watching the crews unloading and loading supplies. I stood there – dockside – looking up at this giant ship I was going to call home for the next six to 12 months. Wow! After all pain and testing I have been through with my Crohn's, the hospitalization and recovery, wondering if I was ever going to finally realize this dream. It was actually happening. What an amazing feeling I had. This dancing contract was going to be a dream come true.

I met with JAR's assistant, who was our 'shore mom', to go through all the forms. She made sure we had all our paperwork, passports, contracts and other assorted items in check. She was our go-to person if we needed anything. She assured my mom and dad - who were there to watch me set sail - that I was in good hands. The time arrived for me to give my hugs and kisses. It really was not goodbye; Remember, I was going to be in port every Saturday and I could make a ship to shore call if there was an emergency. I remember walking onto the gangplank to enter the ship thinking, *"Yippee, here I go!"*

My itinerary went something like this: I set sail on Saturdays from the Port of Miami on the S/S Sunward; mid-week we would change ships to the S/S Southward; and then fly back to Miami from Puerto Rico on Saturday morning only to get back onto the S/S Sunward and do it all over again.

Although the S/S Sunward was one of the smaller ships in NCL's fleet, to me it was huge. There were many passenger decks, but the cast and crew lived on the lower decks. NO porthole, no balcony, no sliding doors. How rude. I am pretty sure we were on the bottom deck or at least it felt that way. A porter carried my steamer trunk to my cabin and there I learned I would be sharing a room with two other gals. At the time our cast had one male singer, one female singer and four dancers. Well, this was going to be interesting - I am an only child and I have never shared a room with anyone let alone a room that was no bigger than 10-foot-by-14-foot wide. There were two bunk beds; a built-in desk area; and a bathroom where you couldn't even stand with your arms stretched out because there was not enough room. Perfect. *I sure hope I like these gals!!* Being the new gal was bad enough, but I was nervous because I had been thrown into this with just a few days notice. It was not like there was an entire cast/crew change where everyone got to learn the ropes together. Nope, I had to get it together as quickly as possible.

Even though I had never been on a ship before, I wanted to do all the things a tourist would do. Go to the Lido deck and watch us anchor away, throw confetti in the air and listen to the crew give the mandatory instructional session on what to do should the ship start to sink. But I couldn't do that; I had to start rehearsals that afternoon. I had but a few days to learn an entire show. Because on Saturday, we would be back in Miami and the girl I was replacing would be on her way out. I had one week to find my way around this giant floating city, make friends with my new roommates, learn an entire show and then perform it for Jean Ann the following Saturday when we were back in port. *Hmm. NO pressure, right?* NO stress, right? I had a busy week ahead of me.

I met some of the cast and before I knew it we set sail. I did get a quick opportunity to stand on deck and watch Miami get smaller and smaller, and fade away into the horizon. I walked around the deck stopping to look at the vastness of the ocean, the blue waters and the clear sky. It was amazing how much nothingness was out there. It was a totally different perspective from standing on the beach looking out into the ocean than being in the water looking back at the land. It made one realize how big our planet really is.

Well, that enjoyment did not last long. A few more of my fellow cast members found me. We did all the introductions and exchanged pleasantries, and started rehearsing at 6 p.m. sharp. I really had no idea how many dances I needed to learn in three short days. Not to mention the cast seamstress needed to alter the costumes and headdresses I would be wearing. So off to wardrobe I went, so much for watching the sun set into the horizon. Does the sun really sizzle when it touches the water? I assumed I would have to wait to find the answer to that question.

I watched the show that night and saw there were four numbers before our break when the comedian, juggler, ventriloquist or some other entertainer would do their thing. Then we would go back on for another number or two, and then perform the finale. The show in general lasted about 90 minutes, and there were two shows. A dinner show and a late night show. Hells Bells! I had a lot to learn. The show was called "*Sea Legs*" and the dance numbers in the show consisted of different themes and genres. Gotta get, Gotta get, Gotta get your Sea Legs!

The costume fitting went smoothly - tighten this, make this smaller/bigger. Easy. I was given multiple pairs of fishnets and my show shoes, but there were no extras of anything, if anyone got a hole in their fishnets, they damn well better know how to fix it. Then, I was off to rehearsal. Oh, boy. I was excited and nervous, and scared and worried. These guys had to rehearse because of a contract change, not because it was a new show. They all knew these numbers. They were not too happy with the gal who decided to leave. This was extra rehearsal time for them. I hope I do not mess things up - I need to get this right. But, crap I had a lot of numbers to learn. And when there are only four dancers on stage at one time, and when one person messes up, it stands out like a sore thumb. So, the team captain began at the beginning and we rehearsed for hours. Some of it was easy, some hard, but mostly just remembering the order of the dances and lyrics always helped.

Tomorrow was about rehearsing in my costumes. During a performance, a dancer might only have 45 SECONDS to change from one costume to another, so everyone had to pre-set their costumes from first to last - one on-top of the other, so you could whip off one and put on the next. Holy crap, new dances, new moves, music and do not forget I am dancing on a moving stage. When the ship lists, so do the dancers!

Rehearsals went smoothly, and I had most of the numbers down. Everyone was so helpful, kind and patient. What a great group! I was getting comfortable with the moves and the timing, which made me feel more at ease. The true test would be opening night. Everyone, including myself, knew I likely would mess up. Most dancers usually do on opening night. The only way they learn is to jump in and just do it.

The easy part about all of this was the make-up, false eyelashes, smiles, flirting, and sass. I had that part down years ago - the stage and the audience was NOT my worry. I did not want to disappoint my new cast members. I wanted to get it right the first time. I wanted them to like me.

Now, remember this was my first night on a cruise ship. There was so much to do, so much to see, so many drinks to drink, so much fun to have! But, I couldn't play too much. I needed to be in tip-top shape for rehearsals. I knew I shouldn't drink with all the medications I was taking. I am sure I read that prescription warning somewhere, but dang the print was SO small! But really who the heck was I kidding? I am on a cruise ship for heaven's sake; I am going to drink on occasion. Well, if memory serves me correctly, I was a good girl my first week or so. I did not want to disappoint anyone! Honestly the hardest part was not the dances, it was finding my way around the ship and getting the feathers and the costumes, and the headdresses on when you are a hot and sweaty mess.

My first week was a blur, there were shows to watch, cruise-staff to meet, ship layout to learn, and learning about the crew bar, and the crew pool. These areas were off limits to passengers; these were our own private staff/crew hideaways. Of course there was exploring the islands, going snorkeling, sunbathing, and getting to know my roommates. All the crew members were so wonderful and helpful, and after a few days I knew my way around. I knew my way to the dining hall, the crew pool area and the bars. Finding your way to the bars was easy, finding your way back to your cabin not so much.

The islands this particular ship stopped at were Nassau, Bahamas and San Juan, Puerto Rico. On the S/S Southward the ship stopped at St. Thomas, US Virgin Islands; Puerto Plata, Dominican Republic; Cozumel, Mexico and every ship had a private island. Oh my! What pure beauty and scenery these islands had to offer. Sure, Boca Raton was beautiful and so were its beaches, but the waters of the Caribbean were about the bluest waters I had ever seen, not to mention the sand was pure white. My most favorite place was Megan's Bay in St. Thomas. It was a place I could have pitched a tent and stayed forever. My roommates were more than happy to show me all the hot beach spots and hideaways on each island, the best places to buy duty-free items, best places to eat and the best bars. This experience was going to be better than I ever imagined.

The first week flew by and before I knew it we were back to the port of Miami and that meant I had to perform for Jean Ann! Finally all my years of hard work, sweat and determination were paying off. I was going to be performing in front of one of the most well-respected producers in the industry. I was a little nervous, but mostly excited! All went smoothly and Jean Ann was very pleased with my performance.

That Saturday flew by. I barely had time to go on shore to call Mom and Dad and tell them about my first week because before I knew it, it was anchors away - and we were off again. That night would be my first official show. I was nervous and excited. All my years of rehearsing, training, classes and performances boiled down to my official opening night!

The show was amazing. There I was on stage - in my skimpy costumes - with the music, the band, the excitement of the MC and the ship's captain who introduced us. This was the life. I never dreamed it would be so fabulous. I did make some mistakes, but that was to be expected. To get paid for doing what I love to do while traveling to gorgeous places, not having to worry about cooking or cleaning or laundry - Pure Heaven!

After three months, the contract I was fulfilling was up and JAR asked if I would like to stay on for another six months. *Hell yes! Don't have to ask me twice!* Up to this point everything was running smoothly. My Crohn's hadn't flared, my steroids were tapering down, and I was losing my moon-face. I knew the ships like the back of my hand. Had a boyfriend (or two) and got to go home once in awhile to spend the afternoon with my mom and dad, and to follow up with my doctors. Well, if all this food and alcohol did not cause a flare up I'm not sure what would.

We were expected to rehearse once or twice a week, otherwise we played, swam, snorkeled, goofed off, sun bathed, drank, and ate everything and anything we wanted. Life was great. One might even say grand; however, there were a few downsides to working on a cruise line. First, there was not any real TV. There was ship TV, not cable TV like we think of today.

They aired the same shows every week and the movie in the ship's theater played for over a month. There was not any way to order a pizza: one couldn't just get in a car and go for a drive when they wanted to. One got used to the fact that Monday night was pasta night and Tuesday was seafood night. Even though this was the life, after awhile it got a little boring. *Did I really just say that?!* I spent the next six months with a wonderful cast and crew, and we had the best times imaginable. And to this day, I remain friends with most of them.

Today, the ships' entertainment are structured differently. Each ship has its own cast (meaning they do not travel between ships) and the dancers are required to work during the day. Not like the early '80s when we just did our thing and then did nothing. When I look back through my old photo albums I smile and giggle. I wonder what I was thinking with my big hair, crazy outfits and strange poses! But, I would not have changed a thing.

We were given a few free cruise passes, so my mom and dad were able to take a cruise and see me perform. I remember they went on the S/S Southward: It was a seven-day cruise with a much better itinerary. I showed them around the islands and took them to the best little hideaway places I knew. I asked the captain and we got to sit at HIS table for dinner one night. I clearly remember when they came to see the show: Mom reached over to Daddy and covered his eyes when I turned around as there was not anything covering my ass.

JAR had many shows throughout the US and Europe. The cruise line was just one of the many opportunities. As the end of my contract neared about mid-June 1983, JAR asked if I might be interested in moving to New Orleans to work in a show that was in production there. It was called *"French Quarter Follies."* Wow, never having been to Louisiana before, I knew this opportunity would be fun. Mardi Gras was something everyone must experience at least once.

TEN

ON TO THE NEXT SHOW

As it turns out, again, I did not have much time to decide if I wanted to accept Jean Ann's offer as she needed someone in New Orleans by Thursday! Yeah, four days from the end of my NCL contract. I discussed this opportunity at length with mom and dad, and all the pros and cons of accepting this gig. The length of the contract was one year and because it was so far away I wouldn't be able to come home on the weekends. My daddy was very much against New Orleans. Dead set against it, actually. But somehow my mom said something that convinced Daddy to let me go, and he finally gave me his blessing. Honestly, I could do whatever I wanted to - I was 18. But, that was not how I was raised. I respected my parents, their beliefs and their values. I always wanted to make them happy and proud of me. They knew how much this next gig meant to me. They also knew how much time (and money) they had spent getting me to this point. So, I told Jean Ann I would accept the contract. This only gave me a few days at home to regroup, and I needed to get in to see my gastroenterologist.

I was still feeling great. I had weaned off the Prednisone and was not taking any medications. My weight was stable, somewhere around 105, which was usual for me. It was hard to imagine I hadn't been sick in almost nine months. I guess with all the excitement and fun of dancing I didn't realize I was not having any issues, pains, swelling, fevers, nothing! All was great and I felt great. The doctor was pleased with my health and suggested we do a follow up colonoscopy when I return from New Orleans. Woo-hoo, I was good to go! During the next few days I tried to catch up with any friends who were still in the area. I visited with family; I went to the beach; I went out dancing and just tried to enjoy some down time - all three days of it.

From what I was told, the gig in New Orleans was very different from the show on the ships. Luckily, housing was provided for us, so I did not have to find an apartment. And, it was furnished, so I did not need to worry about bringing or buying all the items that go into furnishing an apartment. The cast was larger, the show was longer and we performed more often. That was all OK. What was going to be totally different was I needed a totally new wardrobe than what I was used to. Don't think you want to walk around the French Quarter in short shorts, tube tops or other skimpy clothes without standing out like a sore thumb. I had plenty of summer clothes and swim suits, but New Orleans got cool in the winter, and I did not own a lot of clothes that would keep me warm, so a few new clothing items were needed.

Finally, I had all my stuff packed and we headed for the airport and I was off for my next adventure. Who knew what the next year might bring?! All of the travel arrangements were taken care of by JAR. I even had a ride arranged from the airport to downtown. The show was in the Sheraton hotel on Canal Street, which is one of the main streets and one of the perimeter streets to the French Quarter. The cast and crew housing complex was one street into the Quarter and two blocks away from the hotel. There was no need to worry about a vehicle; you were able to walk to and from the show without a problem. Once my flight landed and I arrived downtown with all my worldly possessions, I learned the apartment I was living in was on the 3rd floor (while everyone else lived on the 4th or top floor). No biggie, the 3rd floor apartment was all mine if I wanted it. I did not have to share with anyone. Now this was HUGE, since I spent the last 12 months crammed into a sardine can with two other females. I was more than happy to be alone and not share a dang thing with anyone!

I needed to find the landlords so they could give me my keys, let me into my new place and give me a quick tour. They weren't hard to find, and there really was not any tour, but they did make a point to show me where the fire escapes were. Hmm?

I brought my luggage up three flights of stairs, drug it all down the hall and could not help but wonder, *"Where the heck are the porters? I am used to them helping me. This stinks!"* I unpacked a thing or two, and headed over to the hotel; I was anxious to see the stage and the showroom. Not to mention I am ready to meet the cast and crew, and I am more than ready to go drinking on Bourbon Street!

Now, I have never really been a gal who is scared to go anywhere. I do not mind walking alone, exploring alone. I do not mind getting lost and I am not afraid of people. Maybe it is the old soul in me that just kind of knows when it is OK to do something and when it's not. I exited the apartment building to find it is across the street from a bar called Jim-an-I. This is a bar where some of the local gays and transvestites liked to hang out. Maybe this is what Daddy was so nervous about. Anyway, I walked two blocks to Canal Street and made my way to the hotel.

The hotel was big and elegant. There was a grand entryway with escalators that led up to theater. Once there I found the theater was dark - meaning there was not any cast or crew there. But wow, it was a theater with rows and rows of tables and chairs, and a big stage with curtains and a backdrop. *Oh, how exciting is this going to be!* Since no one was there I figured it would best to go back to my apartment (I had never said that before) and start unpacking. Huh, I had my very own apartment. How cool was this?

I took my time walking back and actually walked the long way. I walked down Canal Street and down Bourbon Street, and wandered up and down some of the side streets. I saw locals, tourists, drunks, bums, gypsies, cops on horseback, bars with girls dancing on poles and transvestites. Well, now these were sights I never saw in any neighborhood in Boca! Actually, I hadn't really ever seen a transvestite before, but damn some of those *ladies* had some awesome legs! I got quite a quick education - no wonder my daddy had reservations about me living there!

I eventually made it back to my apartment and began to unpack and set up house. Not to mention I had to go the grocery store and stock my refrigerator with the foods I was accustomed to eating. Well this should be interesting, I'm not sure if I am a fan of Creole cooking or not. Were all the spices and herbs, and Cajun flavorings they used going to agree with me? Was I going to be able to find the same brands I was used to? But most importantly, I don't really know how to cook. I certainly can't afford to eat out all the time. Well now here is something I hadn't given any thought to. I guess it is a good thing I only eat because I have to, not because I enjoy it. Honestly, sometimes I don't even care if the food is hot.

I was scheduled to meet the cast and crew that night, and watch the show. There were two shows per evening, five nights a week: a dinner show and a late show. I would be performing 10 shows per week vs. three shows per week, like I did on the ships. Good news was we had Monday and Tuesdays off, and better news was I did not have to travel throughout the week (with all my belongings).

Now the hard part - what to wear to meet my future cast mates. I want to make a great impression! For some reason I remember exactly what I wore. It was a short black dress that snapped all the way down the front. I paired it with a red belt and the highest pair of pumps I owned. My hair was long and permed, and I wore it down. I thought I looked great. I was totally tanned and, not to mention, slim and trim.

Once I got to the theater I was greeted by one of the dancers, her piano playing husband, a stagehand, a sound engineer and another dancer. All seemed really nice and friendly, and the sound engineer was rather handsome, if I do say so myself. It was almost show time, and I watched the show from the edge of my seat. I counted all the numbers/dances I would have to learn and I admired the more elaborate costumes and stage sets. After the second show, I met the rest of the cast and crew, and then we all went out for a welcome to the cast party.

After a few rehearsals (a week to be specific) I had the dances down pat. If you remember, I was replacing a dancer who cut their contract short. The official contract change was not scheduled until the end of August. But with any cast change the producer usually comes to pay a visit. When your boss is watching, you darn well better be performing perfectly. Jean Ann was obviously familiar with my dancing and was very pleased with the show and my performance, and told us she would visit again in August.

It didn't take long before I had already done about 100 shows. I was having the time of my life! I spent any free time exploring the city, riding the streetcars, going to the infamous Saenger Theatre, having picnics at the Audubon Zoo and trying each and every restaurant and bar. No wonder my belly was giving me some issues: all the eating and drinking, and partying I was doing might be catching up with me.

I had a boyfriend who was much older than me. His contract was up in August and good thing – he was on bad terms with Jean Ann. I remember missing him and traveling to Los Angeles to visit. I never told my mom and dad I did this. While in Los Angeles he wined and dined me. He took me to see the musical, "*DreamGirls*." Remember the film adaptation starring Jennifer Hudson? He was the man for me. Or at least I thought he was, but really, what did I know? I was 19. Anyone that wines and dines me is the man for me. One thinks they are in love, but everyone knows how those 19-year-old relationship/stories end and eventually this one did, too.

I flew back to New Orleans only to find out I had been robbed. I had never felt so violated in my life. I remember walking down the hallway and seeing my door wide open and looking in to find all my belongings had been strewn everywhere. As it turns out the only thing missing was my boom box. Well, needless to say this experience scared the heck out of me. I did not want to stay by myself. What if it happened again? What if it happened when I was there? I remember calling the police and it took them forever to arrive and take a report. It seemed as though a break-in in the French Quarter was not such a big deal for them. Well, it was for me! It scared the shit out of me!

At this point, I had been in New Orleans about three or four months, and I had become great friends with all the cast and crew. We did everything together. We were a family. We would frequently take off after the late show on Sunday and drive for hours to Biloxi beach, sleep on the beach, listen to music, watch the sunrise and party. The next morning we would make the drive back to New Orleans, stop for a healthy breakfast of bacon, biscuits and pancakes - you know, sponge food. There were usually five or six of us that regularly made the trip. There were usually three or four of us dancers/singers, and two or three crewmembers, one of which was always the handsome sound engineer (Mark) I mentioned before. He and I used to flirt all the time, but then again I flirted with a lot of people. On one particular trip back to the French Quarter, Mark, being the gentleman he was insisted he walk me to my apartment door. He wanted to be sure I was safe, as I did not need to happen upon another break in incident. And, as you can guess, he made sure I was safe and sound.

The next few weeks were a blast. Mark, his roommate and I partied, went out, ate out, saw shows, took drives to the beach and just had an absolutely terrific time. Mark's sister and brother-in-law lived in a nearby parish, and he introduced me to them. My mom and dad came to visit, and we did all the touristy things. They saw the show a few times and mom made us some good old-fashioned, home-cooked meals. She even made me a pot of tuna and noodles. They both liked Mark and were happy that I had someone watching over me!

Now while you might think living in the French Quarter would be fun, it actually wasn't all that great with the constant stream of people and parades, not to mention the noise, lights and the frequent sounds of sirens. I wanted to move and decided to move in with Mark and his friend. Mark lived in an area called "Uptown," which was a much safer neighborhood. Although it was miles from the theater I would be living in a house with a yard. Since I got to live rent free, I was in charge of the grocery shopping, laundry and cleaning the kitchen. There were times when I would have preferred to pay rent! Mark's friends from the Midwest would often visit. I knew (but I didn't really know) he and his high school sweetheart were still dating. Well, she visited once (actually twice) with a group of his friends. Of course, they were going to stay at the house. Well, guess what that meant? Guess who had to move out? Yup, that would be me. Whatever! I knew what I was getting myself into.

It was about this time I started to feel very tired. I chalked it up to the fact that we performed 10 times per week, plus my eating and beverage consumption was over the top. I was not following doctor's orders. I was not being responsible and because of this I was beginning to pay the price. I guess my carefree lifestyle was catching up with me. But the holidays were approaching and it was time to start planning the Christmas party. We all had plans to go to our respective homes for a few days and Mark assured me that when he went home he would not see his girlfriend. *Yeah, yeah, whatever.*

The holidays came and went, and by January 2, 1983 we were back performing. The dynamics of the cast/crew changed often, and we were never without drama. Cast members left, old cast members returned, dance partners changed, numbers were cut and people got injured. There were times when all this drama stressed me out, and that may have been why my gut hurt. There were often days or even weeks that went by when it was hard to eat, or I had pain in my joints and swelling in my legs. All of the prior memories of pain, agony, lethargy and frequent trips to the bathroom came rushing back. It was bad enough having to make a beeline for the bathroom, but to do so in full costume was no easy feat. But the show must go on. Suck it up and remember, NO EX-

CUSES! I never really told anyone (except Mark) about my Crohn's – did not feel they needed to know. With a little minding of my manner, my flare-up ceased. I knew I had been very non-compliant. I needed to scale it back, slow down a little. And within a few weeks, I was feeling better.

The spring months quickly approached and I was excited to experience Mardi Gras. Now, there is a city that knows how to throw a party. Mardi Gras lasts for days with the culmination of one big parade with floats and bands, and krewes. They threw beads and doubloons, and if you flashed them they threw you more! I did not say I did that, I just said that is what happened. During the spring months, Mark and I went to see movies, spent time with friends, laid around and just enjoyed our time together. I do not remember us ever fighting - we just had fun. We totally enjoyed each other's company; it was easy to hangout. We all have one of those friends where you can sit next to each other and do not feel like you have to say a word! I wondered what was going to become of our friendship when my contract ended. And, that was going to happen soon: The end of June, to be exact.

This meant the new cast would be arriving soon and my last few weeks would be spent teaching them the ropes, rehearsing with them, showing them around the city, etc. It was not long before we were performing our last show. There were always some antics during the last show. What are they going to do, fire us? It was always a bittersweet experience. I remember staying an extra day so I could watch the new cast do their thing. They did great and I knew the show could, and would, go on without me.

After packing all my worldly belongings, I said my goodbyes. I saved my last goodbye for Mark. I remember crying and thinking, I wonder if I am ever going to see him again? He still really was involved with the gal from up North, but if life has taught me anything (in all my long 19 years) it was that I knew when things were going to work out and when they were not. Maybe it was the old soul in me that gave me the hunches. I told myself if I did not hear from him within two weeks it was over and my intuition was wrong. *Me, wrong?* Never!

ELEVEN

WHAT COMES NEXT?

I returned to Boca, and tried to relax and unwind after what had been a whirlwind of a year. I contacted my friends that were still in town and went back to doing what I did before I began my dancing career - club dancing, going to the beach, partying and enjoying myself. I followed up with all the doctors as I was instructed to do and they all seemed to think - even though I had been less then compliant - all things seemed to be going well. To be on the safe side, the doctor put me on some medication; well, actually it was taking a lot of medications, but I felt OK and that was all that mattered.

The Florida weather in June was absolutely perfect and I was home. And then, lo and behold, guess who called? Yup, Mark! Bingo - I knew it. We talked for hours and hours. Oh, how I had missed him.

After a few weeks of fun and sun, I realized I needed to find work. I could not go on being a beach bum forever. As I began my search, I happened upon an audition with a company called Miller Reich Productions. They had many national and international musical and revue shows. My timing could not have been more perfect. They were holding auditions mid-July, which happened to be the next week. Remember, I am not nervous about auditions, either I have what they are looking for, or I do not; ultimately nothing to lose and a potential contract to gain. So, I drove to the audition in Fort Lauderdale and was hired on the spot. And guess what? They wanted me to leave in three days. Why in the hell don't these companies plan better? Do they think everyone can just pick up and leave at the drop of a hat? Well, I guess an unemployed dancer can.

The show I auditioned for was in a place called King of Prussia, Pennsylvania, which is 30 minutes East of Philadelphia, near a small historic town called Valley Forge. The show was called *"Follies Royale"* and it was in the Lilly Langtry Lounge of the Sheraton hotel. With a whopping three days to pack, Mom and I once again scrounged around to gather my belongings. The only thing I REALLY needed this time was a winter coat. Try finding one of those in South Florida in July! It is like trying to find a bathing suit in the Midwest during the dead of winter. And, remember the times - this is 1984. There was not any Amazon or online shopping. Hell, I didn't even own a computer!

With everything ready to go, I said my goodbyes and was off again for another adventure. As always, I was excited to arrive at my new destination, meet the cast, see the show and see where I would be living. Not to mention I was kind of excited I would get to experience autumn and winter, as I had never seen the leaves change before.

Upon my arrival I met our stage-mom who showed me around the theater and introduced me to everyone. Holy cow, this theater was even bigger than the Sheraton in New Orleans. This theater was at least four times bigger. It held at least 300 people, and it had a balcony level, too! I learned we were dark (closed) on Mondays and Tuesdays; did two shows on Wednesday, Thursday and Friday nights; and three shows on Saturday and Sunday. Holy crap! That made 12 shows per week! It was a good thing we lived in the hotel where the theater was located!

I was so anxious and excited to watch the show. This show was even bigger than the JAR shows I had been in. There were more elaborate costumes, bigger headdresses, about 15 singers and dancers, and about a dozen crewmembers. Wow, I could not wait to get started! As I got settled in, I began to realize we were in the middle of nowhere. It was not like the French Quarter where you could hop on a trolley or walk downtown; we couldn't go anywhere that was not a 30-minute cab ride. *So, now what the heck do I do with my days off?* It was mid-July and not exactly hot, but still warm enough to sit by the pool. Outside of rehearsal, the days were long and the entertainment options were limited. I quickly became very close friends with everyone in the cast, because all there was to do was hang out in the hotel.

I had 10 days of rehearsals before my first performance. This show was over two hours long. There were a lot of dance numbers, adagios, two intermissions and the grand finale - not to mention plenty of costume changes. Overall, it was a fabulous show. Due to my extensive ballet background, I earned myself an adagio number with a dancer named Tom. We performed a duet from *"Sleeping Beauty"*. The producers also asked if I would be their new model for the shows' newspaper and promotional materials. *Of course I would, I would love to!*

Opening night finally arrived. I was not nervous, just excited! I got a beautiful flower arrangement from Mark for good luck. The shows went well as did the next night's performance and the next, and the next. I had only been dancing in this show for about a month or so before Mark told me he wanted to visit. Yeah! A visit would be fan-tab-u-lous! He was planning on visiting the end of September. That was a few short weeks away. I could hardly wait!

It had been a few months since I had been to the doctors and at this point my body was holding up from a GI standpoint, but from an I can't rehearse anymore standpoint, I was one sore and tired girl. I was so happy I did not have any gut pains, or swelling or diarrhea, or any of the other things I have experienced. It was much easier to be compliant there as there wasn't much to do. I never put two and two together, but now that I think about it, when I followed doctors orders; i.e. didn't drink, eat like crap and got plenty of rest, I felt better. I guess one could say, "I was in remission," and I hoped to stay there!

I wished the days away so Mark would finally be there. He arrived on a Saturday and I had never been so happy to see anyone. He saw the shows and said how great I did and looked. We went out that night and had a blast. The following day - Sunday - turned out to be the best day of my life. Mark - out of the blue - proposed! Totally did not see that coming, but somewhere deep down I knew one day he would. I just did not think it was going be that day. Of course I accepted before he could finish getting the words out of his mouth. Wow, I was going to get married! Holy cow, I could not wait to tell everyone.

After Mark left (he was working for JAR on the NCL's biggest ship, the Norway), the following few months were boring. Seems I resorted back to some of my old habits: I did a lot of drinking, lying around and playing, my new-found favorite, ping-pong. There was the occasional trip to Philly to see a football game and one time I took the train into New York for the night. But overall, it was fairly boring. Watching the seasons change was nice and all, but it was cold and I really was not too fond of this winter weather. My body was tired: 12 shows a week for months on end is taxing. I don't care how young, old or how good of shape one is in - it is just plain hard! December 2, 1984 marked my last "*Follies Royale*" show in the Lily Langtry Theatre in Valley Forge, PA. The cast and crew pulled a few pranks. Of course there was a big party and celebration after the show. Then the next day I found myself on a plane heading back home.

This is becoming a familiar scenario - back to Boca, back to the usual sun and fun and friends, and unemployment. Except this time I will get to see Mark. The Norway docks every Saturday, so in a few short days I will get to see my fiancé!

December in Florida is, as I said before, warm and sunny. But Floridians still go Christmas shopping, put up a Christmas tree and wrap presents. Mark and I planned to exchange our gifts the following Saturday. He was only in port for a few hours, so we could not waste any precious time.

After being home for a few weeks, I began my search for dancing opportunities and as my luck would have it, I found myself auditioning to be a Solid Gold dancer, and once again I got the job. However at our first rehearsal I found out it was a topless show. Well, would have been nice to know that tidbit of information before I even auditioned. This clearly was not going to work, so I declined the gig and continued my search. The holidays came and went, and I was not finding any new job opportunities. Little did I know I would not have to continue the search, as there was a bigger job that had just started brewing.

TWELVE

DING DONG, BELLS ARE RINGING

In January, Mark's brother's wife died of cancer. We flew to Edwardsville (just 20 minutes from downtown St. Louis) for the visitation and funeral. It was cold to say the least. I was not prepared to freeze and I had no idea how to shuffle on the ice and snow since that is what people seem to do so they don't fall flat on their butt, which I did a few times. I also was not ready to meet my future in-laws, especially under these circumstances. Nonetheless, everyone welcomed me and as sad as the event was, I was happy to meet everyone. But, how in the heck do people live up here in this cold, brown, barren area they call the Midwest? All the trees are bare, the sky is always cloudy and it gets dark early. I need sun, palm trees, blue skies and ocean breezes. This place isn't for me.

When we returned to Florida, Mark went back to the ships and I continued to search for a dancing job. January passed, then February was almost over and I'm still just bumming around and enjoying life. But, my gut didn't seem right. Did all the drinking and partying from the last few years finally catch up with me? Oh boy. I put on a few pounds, too, but chalked that up to the fact I went from dancing my ass off doing anywhere from nine to 12 shows a week to laying on the beach doing nothing. So, some weight gain was expected, I suppose. But something was not right. The pains I felt weren't the same as Crohn's pains. It was odd, but I could definitely differentiate between pains. And, these pains were not related to my gut! Then something strange happened, I started growing boobs. I never really had much to speak of in that department and that was OK with me, but now they were growing and they were sore. I really didn't put two and two together, but now I think we know where this scenario is headed. Well, it was easy to narrow down a conception date since Mark was only in port on Saturdays. Doing the math correctly, my due date would be in September. Oh boy, that was six months away!

I tried to pull the wool over my mom's eyes as I attempted to sneak a brown paper bag out of the house. I was headed to the Planned Parenthood clinic to confirm my suspicion. I don't think she saw me. Yeah right! Well, BINGO, I was about 12-weeks pregnant! Interesting how I could be so in tune with my body when I danced, and so out of tune with my body about this. I really had to start paying closer attention.

Amazingly I didn't have any morning sickness. I'm quite lucky from what I hear! Then, I got to thinking about all the partying I did during the holidays and all the falling down on the ice and all the other potential hazards that might be cause for concern. Oh no, was this baby going to be normal?!?

Mom and Dad already knew Mark had proposed and we were planning on getting married later that year, after his contract on the ship was over, but telling them I was three months pregnant was quite another song to sing. However, they took the news well (thinking they suspected long before I suspected that I was pregnant), and the wedding planning process began. Lesson learned from a speedy wedding preparation process is that the less time it takes someone to plan a wedding, the less money spent. We tied the knot on March 29th, 1985: a mere four weeks after I found out I was pregnant. Talk about fast.

Needless to say, the Catholic Church I attended (remember the one with the nuns and the rulers, and catching the snow on our tongues) didn't want to marry us. If we wanted to get married in the church, we had to attend a crash course about marriage. Well, how the heck were we going to do this with Mark only home on Saturdays? But we did it, and we ended up having a traditional church wedding. Everyone in Mark's family made the trip, and a few of his longtime friends did, too. The reception was in the backyard of our Boca house. The day was sunny, the sky was clear blue, and outside of forgetting Mark's belt and the fact I couldn't get his wedding ring over his knuckle, the wedding went off without a hitch.

After a beautiful reception, we headed for Miami because Mark had to get back on board the ship. Yes, he still had to work. So, guess what we did for our honeymoon? We took a cruise! Really! A year was not long enough for me to be on a ship! This really was not what I had envisioned for a honeymoon, but it was what it was and it was what we did.

It was very different being a passenger vs. being staff or crew. More fun, more time to watch the sun set and listen to the waves, and enjoy the pool. But, the living arrangements weren't any different; I stayed in Mark's cabin, which was as tiny as mine used to be. We didn't even have the honeymoon suite. All I remember is I was as happy as I had ever been. Who would have guessed this handsome sound engineer who met me on my first night in New Orleans would end up being my husband and the father of our child? And, to think my daddy didn't want me to go to New Orleans! I learned years later that the night Mark met me he told his friend that he met the girl he was going to marry. Maybe we are both old souls.

So, here we are, back in port the following Saturday and I'm going back to my mom and dad's house, and Mark is setting sail (his contract was not up until September). Well, now this was odd: newly married, pregnant, living at home and unemployed. Wow, wonder what Mark's parents (who didn't really know me at all) thought about this? Regardless, my mom and I did all the things moms and daughters do when planning for the arrival of a baby, and I couldn't wait for my baby shower, not to mention we had to find a place to live.

My aunt owned an apartment complex in Boynton Beach, which was about 15 minutes north of Boca and as luck would have it, there was a two-bedroom apartment available. Perfect. But, what the heck do we put in it? I didn't have any furniture, kitchenware, mirrors, accessories, etc. We really didn't need to move in for a few more months, but I began setting up house anyway. I would visit Mark on the weekends; I went to the doctors for all my prenatal visits; I went to the GI doctor; and I plugged along each day as I got bigger and bigger. Honestly, I didn't enjoy being pregnant. I was used to being thin. I liked to sleep on my belly and I liked to drink alcohol (not going to lie). I believe I gained close to 40 pounds. Holy crap! I had never weighed that much before. I was hoping the baby would weigh 20 pounds when I delivered him/her.

Interestingly I did not have any Crohn's issues during my entire pregnancy. Not one ache, arthritic pain or fever, and I did not have any urgency to use the bathroom. Was the cessation of symptoms related to the pregnancy or was the fact I wasn't beating my body up dancing the answer? Was it a combination of both? As I learned years later, many women with Crohn's often never have issues during their pregnancy. Regardless, I welcomed the relief from my illness.

Since I had just gotten married, I was no longer able to stay on my daddy's insurance plan, which meant all the OB-GYN bills had to be paid out of pocket. So, a sonogram to determine the gender of the baby was not an option as it was an additional charge and money we didn't have.

The months passed quickly, and I felt like the size of a small planet. Summer heat and pregnancy do not mix. Mark's contract was almost over, so before long we could start a normal life together - as a family.

My friends and my mom threw me a baby shower, so we had everything we thought we needed. The only thing missing was the baby and this little thing took its time arriving. Mark and I made two trips to the hospital thinking I was in labor, but I was told each time to go home. The response from the nurse went something like this: "Come back when the pain is 10 times what it is now." What the hell?

Like I said, I wasn't a fan of being pregnant, and I was sure labor was not going to be any different. And, it wasn't. Even though I had gained more weight than I should have, my smaller frame didn't allow me to deliver naturally. So after hours upon hours of contractions and agony, the doctor finally decided to do a caesarian. *Really, this couldn't have been done 35 hours ago?*

I remember being wheeled into the delivery room, yelling back at Mark and my mom we didn't have a girl's name picked out, and my mom yelled back, "Tara!" I do not remember too much about the procedure, but I do remember the nurses waking me to say I had delivered a beautiful baby girl. Tara was born on Sept 13th, 1985 at 8 pounds, 21 inches long.

I was discharged two days later. Wasn't there a manual, Raising A Baby for Dummies, I'm supposed to get? I didn't know what I was doing.

I have always heard one never wakes a sleeping baby, and Tara slept eight hours her very fist night home. Yes, I said eight hours (don't be jealous) - that is just what she did and she did it the next night and the next. Wow, what an easy breezy kiddo she was going to be. She rarely cried, slept like a log, and was just a happy baby. People hear all these horror stories about colic and allergies to formulas, nonstop crying and sleepless nights. Well, we didn't have any of that. I thought this baby thing just might be OK!

The months went by, and Tara and I had a routine. Now, it was time for this mama to find a job and really get back to work. Mark's contract with NCL had ended, and he was now working with a longtime friend at a brokerage firm in Boca selling stocks. Mark had always been a doer not a sitter, so not sure this was the right position for him sitting behind a desk, but it could be lucrative or deadly since employees worked off of commissions. I began looking for a job, something, anything really, and I was certain it was not going to be dancing, since I was not planning on showing my non-showgirl body to anyone - had a little work to do to get back into shape let alone showgirl shape.

THIRTEEN

WHERE DO I GO FROM HERE?

This was the first time in my life when I was not active, and I was not a healthy eater. I don't mean I ate fast food, because I did not, but I didn't really know how to cook. I made (or should I say heated) a lot of frozen entree type meals for Mark and I had absolutely no thoughts at the time about being a vegetarian, let alone a vegan. I ate the occasional hamburger, chicken and seafood. I did live near the ocean and I do remember how good fresh seafood can be. Believe this or not, but I can honestly say I have never eaten a steak - or a bite of steak - in my entire life. There was always just something about the color and texture that was completely unappealing to me. I was not taking any dance classes and I certainly did not workout for the fun of it. Life at this point was about raising my perfectly happy little girl.

When I began job hunting, I really did not have to look any farther than across the street from our apartment complex. There was a dental office and they had an opening for a receptionist. I interviewed and was offered the job despite not having any experience. So why did they hire me? Don't get me wrong - I was thankful for the opportunity - but I have never really had a *job* before. I have never had a 9-5 commitment with a lunch hour; never had to get dressed up for work, so I knew this experience would be interesting! This was all new and unchartered territory for me; a job with a paycheck and taxes; and responsibilities. Holy crap, I have become an adult! The scary part was I was not only responsible for me, I was responsible for raising another human being. I didn't want to mess this up. Remember: NO manual. I really did not know what I was doing.

I actually enjoyed working at the dental office. A 9-5 job was not as bad as I thought it was going to be. Maybe it was the job, my co-workers or the routine, but I liked it and it helped pay the bills. I didn't have any reason to complain - life really was great. Everything was like I thought it would be; loved my husband, daughter and work. My health was good, sun was always shining and the weather always warm. I had all the responsibilities of being an adult, leading a full and happy life. What more could a girl want?

My Crohn's was at bay, I wasn't following any specific dietary guidelines and I did enjoy the occasional glass of wine. I tried to control any stress and I tried to get a good night's rest. Months went by before I started having belly issues. Mark had never really seen me sick before. He knows me as a strong, full of energy, happy, carefree, fly by the seat of my pants kind of gal; not someone who winces, complains or cries. The time when I was at my worst was when I was diagnosed. I was not about to turn into a gooey mess in front of him now. So, I hid any aches and pains I had. You know - NO EXCUSES. Well, things kept getting worse and I was having trouble eating and started to lose some weight. Then all the symptoms I had when I first got sick started coming back. And as an added bonus I experienced a few new symptoms as well! It was really quite embarrassing to be a newlywed and not want to be intimate with your husband. But the thought and fear I might "have an accident" was mortifying. No way am I going to put myself in that situation, so I called the doctor and he reminded me I was due for my colonoscopy. *Oh Yea!*

We scheduled the appointment and as always the preparation was awful. I was not sure what they were going to find since I didn't feel that great. Well lucky me, they found lots of ulcerations and inflammation. In addition, I had formed what they call a fistula: an abnormal connection between two areas that are not supposed to be connected. No wonder why it hurt like the dickens when I went to the bathroom. I didn't think that felt right, but what did I know.

Apparently, the only remedy for a fistula is surgery! So, now I needed to go see a proctologist who deals with issues of the rectum. Good God - who wakes up one day and says, *"Oh, I think I'll become a proctologist when I grow up?"* Sure I had my share of wardrobe malfunctions while dancing and it is always humiliating to fall on stage when performing in front of hundreds of people, but to lay - face down - on an exam table with one's ass up in the air and a giant bright light shining down on their bum while four to five nurses assist the doctor who is poking around and performing reconstruction surgery...that, my friend, is the epitome of humiliation. *Good grief, what else is this disease going to do to me?*

I survived the surgery, but I was really unaware and unprepared for what the post-instructions involved. I never in my wildest dreams thought what I was told to do by the doctors would ever happen to me. I was told that when I had to "go," I had to go in a bathtub filled with warm water - until my incisions healed. For the love, are you kidding me? Shoot me now, I don't let people see me in pain, so there is no way in hell I'm going to let my new husband see me do this, not in a million. I would rather not eat so I don't have to *go*, then eat and have to *go* in a bathtub. So as one might guess, I limited my food intake for a few days until I healed and I could *go* sitting on the toilet like a normal person.

Once this lovely experience was over and I had my follow up visit, I was put on some additional medications and the doctor increased the dosage of my current medications. It is funny, but as one goes through their daily routine, they become so accustomed to the norm that they forget the way they feel is not normal at all. I look back and realize I was having such regular aches and pains and joint issues, and swelling and other assorted symptomatic Crohn's problems every day. I just got used to them, so it felt normal to hurt. It was not unusual to go to the bathroom five, 10 - sometimes 15 - times a day. It was just the way it was; it was just the way I thought it was supposed to be. I was never told any differently; how was I to know? Road trips were never an option and anytime we went out to a restaurant or somewhere like a mall, the first thing I scoped out was where the restrooms were. Now that I think back, how sad is that? But, ask anyone with Crohn's and they will tell you that it is the first thing they do; it is a vital piece of information someone with Crohn's needs to know!

Once I was completely healed, it was back to work. I really liked working at the dental office. It was close to home, I got my teeth cleaned for free and the girls I worked with were great. Well, except for one. There always seems to be one co-worker who has their panties in a wad. I am not really sure why I stopped working there. I know I was not let go, so I guess I must have quit.

The next job I remember having was at the same brokerage firm with Mark. As much as I loved him, this was a lot of togetherness, but it seemed to work. I will admit, it was hard watching some of the more aggressive brokers bring in big buy tickets, which meant big commissions while Mark brought in smaller tickets or none at all which meant little commissions or nothing. We both knew this was not the right job for him, but it is what we did at the time.

Our weekends were spent with our friends from the firm, or we would take Tara to the pool or beach. Tara was such a joy to raise, we could not have asked for a more perfect little girl. It was fun to dress her up and my mom and dad spared no expense in buying her new and pretty things. I'm thinking they pretty much knew they were only getting one grandchild.

FOURTEEN

TIME TO MAKE THE MOVE

We continued with this routine for the next few years, until the brokerage firm we worked for decided they were going to open a branch in Edwardsville, IL (the town where Mark grew up). This was a big decision for us. My parents and family were here in Boca. His parents and family were there in Edwardsville. Tara was three at the time, and at that age she was so much fun - a self-sufficient, independent little angel. How can one just pick up and move across the country? My mom and dad were much older than Mark's parents and Tara was the apple of my folk's eye. It was a very hard decision to make.

After what was months of discussing our options we made the decision we were going to move to the Midwest. Oh, boy! What was I getting myself into? I didn't like the cold and I would miss my folks terribly, but it was what we needed to do. It was decided we would stay with Mark's mom and dad until we found our own place – our very own house! I was going to become a homeowner, with a mortgage and taxes, and insurance and headaches. The hardest part about this move was the new office was opening the beginning of January, which meant we needed to leave right before Christmas. Wow, this was going to be tough!

We hired a moving company to move all our belongings across the country. I spent as much time as I could that December with my folks so they could spend as much time as they could with Tara. How do you tell a three-year-old she is moving away from everything and everyone she has ever known?

The day finally arrived for the moving van to pack up our things, put our suitcases in our car and make our way across the states to cold country. I watched as the movers took our boxes marked fragile (hell, we didn't have anything fragile) and load them into the semi. This was it: we were out of there. We said our final goodbyes to my parents and family, and friends and started on the road.

We arrived in Edwardsville two days before Christmas, and like I said we were going to be staying with Mark's mom and dad. Well, I had NO idea what to expect or what I was getting myself into. I had been to their house the January before for Mark's sister-in-law's funeral, but now it was the holidays; a happy and joyous time, and the Huntley's spared no expense in decorating their home inside and out.

It was decided the three of us were going to stay on the third floor, Mark's old room. It had ample space and a small studio type kitchen. All of our other worldly belongings, once they arrived, would go into storage until we found our own home.

OK, so here I am with Tara, in this giant house, with family she and I don't know and all the goings-on of the holidays. Hell, I'm overwhelmed so I can't even imagine how Tara must feel! You see the holidays, especially Christmas Eve, were very big occasions in the Huntley household. It involved days of food preparation with the culmination of a formal Christmas Eve dinner. The family also attended midnight mass and then would return home to enjoy the annual reading of the "*Littlest Angel*" and a few other books and passages. Then, we would send the young ones upstairs to bed, and the adults would turn into Christmas elves and hang the stockings, bring the presents down and place them under the tree. There were so many gifts that they literally covered half of the living room floor. Remember, Mark has three other brothers and a sister, most of whom have spouses and children. There were more presents there then I had ever seen! On Christmas morning, the tradition was that everyone would line up in age order and march down the stairs. Each sibling had their own designated couch where they sat and opened all the beautifully wrapped presents. Once all the ooh'ing and thank you's were said, David (Mark's dad) would cook a big breakfast and we would sit around the dining table, and enjoy our breakfast brunch. I think Mimosa's may have been involved, too!

Good grief, this was overwhelming! My family in Boca had our traditions, too, but there were only the three of us, so I had never experienced anything like this! Because we arrived a few days before Christmas, I was not there in time to help with the food preparation (which was likely a good thing seeing how I had no clue how to make anything) but I was able to help with the clean up and wash the dishes. So, I pitched in where I could. I wanted my new in-laws to like me. I wanted to make a good impression. I did not want to disappoint anyone. Tara was a shoe-in; she was three, smart as a tack and cute as a button.

The week between Christmas and New Year's Day was spent unpacking, driving around town trying to find a home and getting together with any of Mark's friends that happened to be in town for the holidays. Mark's sister and family left around the first of the year and the opening of the brokerage firm was quickly approaching. Not to mention we needed to find a daycare for Tara. Luckily with David being employed at SIUE, we were able to get her on the waiting list for the Early Childhood Center and as luck would have it, we did not have to wait long. But that was going to be another expense we needed to add into our ever-growing budget.

Even though there had been much change, my Crohn's seemed to be under control. If this move hadn't stressed me out, I'm not sure what would.

Mark and I asked a long-time family friend/realtor to help us find a place to live. I was not familiar with the town at all, but the elementary, middle and high schools were about a half-mile apart from each other, so the north end of town is where we looked. We saw many homes, but honestly we were not sure how we would be able to pay all the bills. We spent three months looking at homes before we found a place we both liked and was in close proximity to the schools. One must remember, I am coming from sunshine, palm trees, adobe homes with slate tile roofs and pools in just about every yard. All I saw here was dead trees, brick or stucco-type homes and shingled roofs.

It snowed my first few weeks there, and being totally unfamiliar with winter protocol I had a lot to learn. For example, you cannot slam on your brakes at the last minute, lest you crash into whatever is around you. Or you had to warm up your car and scrape the windshield otherwise you were not going anywhere until your car thawed. Or dressing in layers was a much better way to keep you warm then throwing on a waist jacket over a lightweight shirt. And, what is it with long johns? They must be the ugliest things I have ever seen (but come to find out they do keep you quite warm). Also, I was unaware they spread rock salt on the roads to prevent the roads and bridges from freezing. Well, rock salt makes a dark car look all dirty.

So one day I decided I needed to wash the salt off my car. I pulled it down Mark's mom and dad's driveway, unraveled the hose, got a bucket and sponge and some soap and began spraying the car off. After a few short moments the water pressure came to a screeching halt, but I could still feel the pressure in the hose. *What the heck?! Why wasn't this hose working??? Well, hells bells.* No one was home to help, so I tried one more time to get the water to spray out of the nozzle. Nothing. *OK fine, apparently I'm not supposed to wash my car today.*

When David came home from a long day at the university (he was the Director of University Museums and eventually the curator of the Art department at SIUE), he liked to tinker in the basement on different projects, create new works of art or fix whatever needed to be fixed. Mary Deane arrived home about the same time from her position as Director of the Hayner Public Library in Alton. Well...all hell soon broke loose when David went down to the basement to work and found the basement floor flooded! After running frantically around trying to see if there were any broken pipes or overflowing toilets – which there was not – he asked if I knew or heard anything pop since I was home. I explained I did not hear anything unusual, and then casually mentioned I did try to wash my car. It was dirty you see and it needed a bath. Oh my, you should have seen the look on this man's face. I was afraid, very afraid. Well there went trying to win any brownie points with that man! Apparently, in this cold tundra I now live in you *do not wash your car with a garden hose in the middle of winter.* How in the sam hell was I supposed to know that any water left in the hose freezes preventing water from coming out of the nozzle? Really, I'm a Florida girl. I do not know this tidbit of apparently handy information. We don't have prolonged periods of cold weather; we don't have frozen hoses; we don't have to use these things called storm windows; and we certainly did not have to worry spreading rock salt on the roads. How was I supposed to know not to do this? No one told me! And I'm not a mind-reader. Well, luckily nothing was ruined. Needless to say I learned that the carwash is your friend and you never wash your car when the temperatures fall below freezing as the car doors and windows can become frozen shut. What else did I not get the memo on of things not to do in the Midwest? I need to know so I don't piss off the in-laws again.

Even though this act of ignorance provided much conversation for the family, there are many other incidences in which I was able to provide comic relief as well. It was OK and I didn't mind. Actually, some of the things I did were really – just dumb! Sometimes common sense is not quite so common.

OK, back to the house hunting. The brokerage firm had been open for a few weeks now and it had been almost two months that we had been staying at Mark's parents' house; it was time to move on. They were very kind and gracious, and patient, but I'm sure we were cramping their style. Not to mention I felt like I had to walk on eggshells and could not be myself. One day we came across a house that was in foreclosure. It was a two-story red brick house with a basement. Ha! Now that is funny - I was going to have a house with a basement!

We put in a bid, it was accepted and soon we would be signing the mortgage papers, and we could call ourselves homeowners. The outside of the house was OK, but the inside walls were made from something called plaster and lathe?!? *OK, I'll go with it.* The entire house needed to be cleaned before we moved in, so lots to do. Then we had to move our belongings into a two-story house with more rooms on the first floor than we had in our entire two-bedroom apartment. Needless to say, the rooms looked bare. But I guess that is how every couple starts out. Right?

Our lives seemed to be going in the right direction: We were both employed; Tara was settling in and enjoying daycare; I was making friends and we were working on the house. And by this I mean Mark was working on the house. He gutted a room; I designed it; and he rebuilt it. Now I see Mark's true passion was not soliciting on the phone behind some desk, but working with his hands - creating! And he was really quite good at it. Not sure how much longer he stayed with the brokerage firm, but I do remember his brother got him a job at the local nursery/landscape facility. Now this was right up his alley. He got to meet with customers, design their landscaping and then install (plant) it. Shovels, power tools and work boots were much more his style and speed, not dress pants/shoes/shirts and ties. Not to mention, I was not a fan of ironing!

We had been in Edwardsville for about six months and it was time for me to establish myself with a few doctors. Thank goodness I was feeling fine. I didn't want to run the risk of having a flare-up and not have a doctor to call upon. I took Mary Deane's recommendations and went to her doctors. Surprisingly, I liked them all. My initial visits - due to my lengthy health history - took a while. And, of course, it was time for another dreaded colonoscopy. It was time to tell if the current medications I was taking were working. However, the test results showed I continued to have some sort of inflammation. I struggled to understand how the results could show so many areas of inflammation and I didn't feel badly. Was I really so accustomed to tolerating pain. This can't possibly be a good thing. I think I need to learn to become more aware of my body and how it is performing. The new doctor adjusted my current medication regimen; let's see if the change makes a difference.

At this point - married four years, Mark began to realize he needed to look for signs that I did not feel good such as moving slowly due to arthritis; inability to open a lid on a jar; inability to bend my elbow enough so I could brush my hair or my teeth; swelling in my ankles or hands; redness in my eyes; arms crossed over my belly; frequent trips to the bathroom; general tiredness - all these things. He figured out I was never going to tell him I didn't feel good. It was only when I really hurt would I want to snuggle up and have him put his arms around me. That usually meant I felt like shit. I'm not a touchy, feely, hold my hand and let's skip kind of person. Never have been! So if I wanted a hug, something was up!

I did have a flare-up in the early '90s and I remember being admitted to Barnes Jewish Christian (BJC) hospital. I was hooked up to an IV and the doctors ran test after test and the nurses constantly took my temperature or drew blood or woke me up for something. The docs tried some of the newer classes of medications, but sometimes the old standbys just worked best. I remember that hospital stay because I was sharing a room with a young girl, who was maybe 16, and she was in because the doctors were reversing her colostomy bag. OMG! I was never so afraid in my life. Even though I had spent the better part of the last six years in pain of some sort, and on various medications, I never had to have any surgery to remove part of my intestines, let alone go through something as traumatic as getting a colostomy bag. I was truly lucky! *Oh, thank you God I'm not in this girl's shoes.* How awful it must be to go to school with a colostomy bag, or worse, go on a date.

You know when you are really afraid of something you bargain with God. You say something like, "If you help me through this...I promise I won't ever..." Well, I did just that: I prayed that when I was released from the hospital I would start being more compliant. I never ever wanted to have surgery let alone have this disease go so far that I needed a colostomy. This was truly a huge wake up call for me.

My mom and dad came up for a visit shortly after I was released from the hospital. I clearly remember it was the Christmas holiday, it was very cold and we were experiencing lots of ice. Driving in these conditions was challenging to say the least. I succeeded in taking out our driveway fence a few times that winter.

This was the same year Santa brought Tara a puppy for Christmas. This dog was a mutt, but resembled a golden retriever and a lab. Tara was about four, so being the Disney fanatic she was, she chose Pluto as the puppy's name. He really was a cutie, a rather energetic little puppy. I thought, We will see how well this works out. I never had a dog before - really didn't need something else to clean up after, and really was not going to be walking him in 20-degree temperatures. So, it was interesting to see who stepped up to the plate to take care of this furry little guy.

I was still working at the brokerage firm. It was easy work and I enjoyed it. Mark was at the nursery, although they don't do a lot of landscaping during the winter (apparently the ground freezes making digging in the dirt a futile effort), which gave him some down time to work on other projects around our house.

Tara went to the Early Childhood Center and enjoyed her time with her friends. Seemed all was going along smoothly. Winter turned into spring and I was thrilled for warmer temperatures. Not sure I was ever going to get used to this winter cold weather stuff. Made me think back to the Christmas cards of us in bikini's sitting in our lounge chairs with a cardboard cut-out Santa Claus, realizing now that was not so nice to send to those shivering in the North. It is much different being on the receiving end of that card!

My health was good and I was being a compliant patient. Much easier when you do what you are told. I had been experimenting with different foods and determining how they made me feel. I did eat some fish and chicken, but no red meat, pork or fast food (i.e. frozen dinners etc.): Those just did not agree with me. The fat content in the processed foods was quite the mover and shaker for me; and the density of meat was really hard to digest. All dairy items seemed to agree with me regardless of the fat content or consistency. Good thing because this Italian loved her cheese! I realized I mostly tolerated cooked veggies vs. raw and all fruits seemed to digest without difficulty. I was not a big fan of legumes, or any bean for that matter, and there certainly were not a lot of soy foods (processed or natural) available then as there are now. I liked, and ate my share of, grains. Potatoes, rice and breads were often my go-to staple. They were not too dense to digest and I really enjoyed lasagna or spaghetti. I did try to cut back on the alcohol. That always seemed to make my gut feel like it was on fire. I was slowly beginning to arrive at some correlations between foods and my physical health. *Why didn't I do this year's ago?*

At this point I also started doing some exercising (walking, biking and the occasional aerobic class). It felt good to move again and I liked the way it made my body look and feel. Now mind you this was purely sporadic, I didn't have a formal plan or program I followed. If the mood struck, I did it.

That summer Mark's entire family decided to take a trip to Wrightsville Beach, NC. *YEAH, I get to go to the beach!* We rented a beach house and spent an entire week playing in the ocean, sightseeing and relaxing. I had never been to the beaches along the mid-coast states before and they were quite different from the beaches of South Florida, but it was a beach and I loved digging my feet into the sand, and I loved feeling the waves surround me. This was as close to the real thing as I was going to get.

When we returned from vacation, it was time to get Tara ready for first grade. Wow! Where did the years go? We enrolled her in N.O. Nelson Elementary School (a half block from our home), purchased all her supplies and started discussing with her what school would be like. She was ready and excited.

I was still at the brokerage firm, but found out the Fairview Heights branch was going to be closing. Relocating with the company was not an option so the search began for a new job. Hmm. Jobs! I did not like jobs - I wanted a career like I had with dancing. I realize a job is a means to an end. Without a job there is no money to pay the bills, so hi-ho, hi-ho it is off to find another job I go. I happened upon a dental office in a nearby town that was fairly new and they were looking for a front office assistant. It was closer to home and the pay was comparable. So I applied since I had prior dental office experience. I was hired and began working full-time. It was a great atmosphere, the dentist was very easy to work for and the office girls were a lot of fun. This started the next phase in my life. Which, as it turns out, is the phase that brought about much change.

FIFTEEN

CHANGES

During the holidays, my daddy would come to visit. He would stay with us for a month or so and at the beginning of the year head back to Boca. The year of 1992 was no different. During the winter months, Mark spent a lot of time working on our home projects. He remodeled the kitchen, made a dining room table base and used the heaviest piece of beveled glass we could find for the tabletop. He worked on other odds and ends for us as well as for our friends and family until the weather broke, spring sprang and then it was back to the nursery, as everyone always wanted new landscaping for the spring.

On March 29th, we had been married for seven years! *Really, seven?* That flew by. We did not take many vacations; we spent our pennies on remodeling our home. An older brick house always seemed to have something that needed attention. And it did not help I wanted him to start on new projects, such as install skylights and finish the basement making it into a bar and workout area.

My Crohn's seemed to be under control. Seems it had been about a year since I had had much trouble. This was nice; I could get used to this, but I did notice that I started getting laryngitis a lot. I always attributed it to the cold weather or to the fact I was too lazy to dress in layers.

Spring seemed to fly by and before I knew it I was having some belly issues. It was always a surprise the way I could flare without warning. There usually were some signs I did not feel good, but they were consistent signs, nothing hurt so badly that it brought me to my knees. So, when I did flare to the point where I could not move, eat, drink or sleep, it was time to see the doctor, who after doing all the lab work and other assorted testing, admitted me to the hospital, again! Seriously, can't we do this with stronger medications? Nope, I had to get infusions, intravenous medications and some types of assorted scans. How bad were my labs and tests that it earned me a one- way ticket to the hospital? How was it I could continue to be so oblivious to the way my body feels? How could I be so out of tune with myself? I thought I was doing better as I was trying to be more compliant. I was trying to eat a little better. I was trying to do some exercise. Maybe I was making the wrong choices; maybe I wasn't doing enough. I wasn't sure and I was uncertain on what to do next.

Some way to spend the month of May, not to mention, if I did not work I did not get paid. And, to top it off, my doctor would not let me go back to work until I had my follow-up appointment and spent two full weeks at home resting. Since they increased my steroid regimen I was told I could eat whatever I tolerated. What the hell does that mean? What kind of instructions are those? Why was I not receiving more specific guidelines? Now that I think back, I never ever once either saw a dietitian while I was in the hospital nor was I referred to one after I was discharged. Heck, for that matter, I wasn't even given written guidelines or a list of foods to choose from or foods to avoid. Something was not right with this picture.

As a result of the most recent flare up, I started having some issues with redness in my eyes, so I needed to see an eye specialist. This is yet another symptom of Crohn's disease that I had not had the pleasure of experiencing before. A symptom of the Crohn's that all stems from a deficient autoimmune system. The eye doctors were able to do some laser type treatments for me, but I still looked like I had pink eye - honestly an eye patch would have been more pleasant to look at than my swollen eye.

Summer was quickly approaching, which meant school would be letting out. I was told at the dental office that they would be cutting back my hours (they were thinking about moving away from the area). So, here I am, not feeling great, taking high doses of steroids, and only working a few days a week. I guess it is time to revise my resume and start looking for yet another job. But wait, my resume consisted mostly of dancing gigs, the job at the dental office in Florida, and my job at the brokerage firm. I began to realize I did not have a lot of professional skills and my work experience was in two totally different fields. Finding a job was going to be tough!

Tara and I spent the summer months going to the pool, library or the movies. She occasionally went to her friends' houses and I occasionally went to the YMCA to take an aerobics class. It made me feel better because the steroids gave me such edgy energy; I needed something to release all of my tension. Mark not only worked at the nursery, he was also doing many side remodeling jobs. Summer flew by and somehow we were able to save some money so that Tara and I could take a trip to Boca to visit Daddy, our friends and family, and old neighbors. She and I were so excited to go. We had a great time and we even took one of those early morning drives to Orlando to see Disney World. Tara enjoyed the Magic Kingdom immensely, although I must admit she was a little afraid of some of the characters and the rides. And, it was much harder for Daddy to get around, as he was now 81 years old. Regardless, we had a fantastic time.

When we returned home to Edwardsville, we were left with a mere month to get Tara registered for school and we still had a short weekend trip to Memphis planned to visit with Mark's sister and family. School started according to plan with Tara dressed in the cutest new outfit with her matching backpack and lunchbox. She also wanted to be part of the Girl Scout/Brownie troop, so we signed up for that as well. It actually was kind of nice I was only working part-time because it did allow me the time to be a "room mom" and to go with her and her class on field trips. That was the fun part, but I'm not sure the stress of only working part-time, with the uncertainty of being let go, was good for my Crohn's as I started feeling a little sick again. Stomach pains were here and there. But, I carried on; NO EXCUSES! I was still taking steroids, granted I was down to 7.5 mg daily which is a far cry from where I started with 60 mg. But they should have been doing the trick and it hadn't been that long since I had my last flare up.

Tara's seventh birthday was approaching and there was a lot to do, as she wanted to have two separate parties - one for the family and the other for her friends. Back in those days, I actually thought it was fun to make fancy cartoon cakes. But, whom was I kidding? I stunk at that AND at making Halloween costumes. Susie homemaker I am not. My trials and errors at making crafty items again provided the family with much to talk about.

The next few months were uneventful - school, work and the occasional aerobic class when my body felt well enough, and then the holidays.

Something else I thought would be really fun to do was buy a REAL Christmas tree. What the hell was this hoopla about? I'm buying a dead tree only to decorate it with lights and ornaments so I can sit and look at its beauty for a few weeks, then take off all of the lights and ornaments, and lug this hard, piney, sticky giant tree stub out of the house, only to step on pine needles for the next few months. Kind of like the green plastic grass from the Easter baskets. How is it you can find that stuff in the middle of June? Well, a few years of the real Christmas tree and its smell were enough for me. Find me the year-end clearance Christmas tree sale: I want a fake tree and I'll buy a can of pine-scented spray to use and fool everyone.

This year brought me the newfound confidence to audition for a few local shows. My weight was back to showgirl weight and I was exercising (well, taking aerobic classes). I was active, and dancing, to me, was like riding a bike. I could just do it! Show me the moves and I'm on it! I auditioned for a local outdoor theater group, but it required some singing and I sang about as well as I made fancy cartoon cakes. I did audition for and do a few gigs with Show-To-Go Productions and COCA, and I actually got to perform on the Fox Theater stage a few times, but that was as far as my dancing was going to take me. Apparently my "old" body was not up for the challenge and the stress of rehearsals and getting all the moves right put me back into a flare-up. Good golly, was this the roller coaster my life was up against forever?

It was about this time I was finally let-go of my job with the dental office. The dentist and his family decided they were going to move away, so now what was I going to do? Well, first off I was going to enjoy a few months of rest, maybe that is what I needed to keep any gut pains away and surprisingly I didn't have any pains or aches over the course of the next few months. This was all good and fine, but I was not working, and I was not bringing in any money. I needed to do something with my life, but what? I knew dancing was not going to be the answer, so I either needed to start looking for employment or maybe go to college. What would I study? If I could be anything I wanted to be what would I be? A teacher? A nurse? A therapist? *Hmm...college.* I was almost 30 years old and I didn't know what I wanted to be when I grew up. Not to mention, if I went to college full-time, when would I work?

If you remember, I did take a few college classes at FAU during my senior year of high school, but there was not any kind of credit that would or could transfer after all these years, so if I did decide to go to college I had to start from scratch! Over the next few months, I would ponder what to do as I lay out by the pool. Did I want to work with numbers (accounting, etc)? No, way. That sounded too hard. Did I want to work with animals? Nope. Even though we had a dog, I really was not what one would call an animal lover. Did I want to work with children? Nope. I did not feel I had the patience to do that. Did I want to teach dancing? Nope. It would frustrate me if the students didn't get it right the first time. Did I want to sell something? Nope. I didn't like asking people to buy things or put them on the spot. Well, at least I had narrowed down the things I did not want to do. What was left? Well, I was a people person so let's work with adults, but in what capacity? What did I have to offer or share with people that could benefit and help them? I pondered this question for many months and then it hit me! I realized over the course of the last few years when I paid more attention to how I ate, it affected how I felt. If I made healthier choices my Crohn's was not so bad. I did not seem to have as many flare-ups when my food selections were better. OK, there was a correlation there. If I can better manage my disease through proper (or healthier) nutrition, then I am sure others can do the same. That's it! I decided to study nutrition and earn a degree in dietetics!

SIXTEEN

COLLEGE BOUND

The decision to go to college was really not hard to make. Once I thought about it, the answer was right there in front of me. Now, I needed to find a school that offered a degree in nutrition. The only in-state schools were ISU (Illinois State University), SIU-Carbondale (Southern Illinois University) and some school near Chicago, but moving was not an option and commuting three hours per day didn't really work either. I decided to shift my search to Missouri schools. As luck would have it, there were a few options. The more I explored, the more I began to realize how expensive college was. If I was going to do this, then I was going to do it as a full-time student. I was pushing 30, and I did not have the time to take a class here and there. Well, I could have gone that route, but remember, I'm black or white, NO gray.

After careful planning and a lot of consideration, Mark and I decided I would take all my general-education classes at SIU-Edwardsville. It was right here in my backyard and all class credits would eventually transfer. Not to mention the tuition was about half of what it was going to cost at Fontbonne College (where I would ultimately enroll for my nutrition degree). Remember, I was starting from scratch, as in it was so long ago that I took any classes I had to take a 099 math class before I could register for the 101 level math class. Remedial math! Now that is funny, I don't care who you are! So, SIUE, *"Here I come."* I took all the appropriate measures to get myself registered and enrolled so I could get this 099-math class out of the way during the summer. Then, in the fall I could begin with all the required general education classes.

I was considered a non-traditional student. In other words, an older student! Honestly, it was quite comical to sit and listen to the 19 and 20 year olds talk about staying out late and how many responsibilities they had. *Really Scooter? Responsibilities?* Try this on for size - I just made a life-changing decision to go to school at the age of 30, which meant I was not going to be contributing financially, I'm married, and I have an 8-year-old daughter to get to and from school/brownies, etc. I have a house to clean, grocery shopping to do, dinners to make, laundry to do...and now I will have homework and tests to study for...shall I continue? *And, you have responsibilities? Bite me!*

I remember getting my very first syllabus. It had all the dates, projects, homework and other requirements that I was expected to complete over the course of the next few months. I wanted to get home as quickly as possible so I could get started. I had homework! It sounded fun and strange to say, but I was actually excited to get started. I loved having deadlines and timelines, and structure. I also registered for fall classes and had a full load (18 credit hours). Wow, this was going to be fun, or the craziest idea I have ever had!

During the summer, while I was taking my basic math class, I did the occasional dancing gig, and I did a little modeling, which helped bring in some money, but it was not anything much to speak of. Overall, any spare time I had during the summer was spent poolside with Tara or going to fun places like the Science Center, Grant's Farm or Splash City.

August arrived and both Tara and I were off to school. Tara loved school, and I am so glad I never had to nag her to do her homework or study. Classes for me went fairly well. I struggled a little with some of the chemistry, but most of the other classes were great. It is always amazing to me that just when a semester starts it is time to register for the next semester. Wow, I'm glad there are advisors to help with all this planning. Fall came and went; I studied, did all my parental duties, did all my domestic duties, took the occasional aerobics class and attended all of Tara's events. My health seemed to be fair and I think my body actually looked forward to the aerobic classes.

That was until the beginning of 1994 when I had a follow-up appointment with my gastroenterologist. Apparently, a pattern was beginning to form. I either overlooked the signs of a Crohn's flare, or I sucked it up and carried on. My body - or at least my gut - was apparently worse off than I thought. Blood test results never lie (kind of like telling the dentist you floss - they know you don't). So, I was put on another round of steroids to reduce any inflammation and to help with any aches and pains I, apparently, was having.

If I break life down, I guess one could say I had a lot on my plate. But it really didn't feel like a lot and I thought I was handling everything really well.

Springtime meant finals and report cards weren't far away, and there were high hopes of relaxing for a few months. As soon as our weather turned a little warmer, my daddy came to visit. He stayed for a few weeks and we enjoyed our time together. Mark's sister and our nieces visited, too. Tara was, of course, very excited to have her cousins in town.

Random thought: A funny thing about living in the Midwest is that time seems to go by faster. I frequently found myself saying, "It is summer again"; "It is winter again"; "It is Halloween again." The weather in Illinois is so different from Florida where it is sunny 24/7 and the trees and grass are always green, and the temperatures always above 80 degrees.

I did start doing something new that spring. I started jogging. It seems while I enjoyed the aerobic classes I needed something else more challenging. I had NEVER jogged a day in my life, so I started out slowly and eventually worked up to three to four miles a few times a week. I would not call myself a runner; I was a person who ran. I did not participate in any events or races; I didn't go out and buy lots of fancy running gear; I just enjoyed this activity as it made me feel more energized, free and in control, not to mention, I liked how my body felt and looked.

Spring semester ended and I was planning on taking the summer off to spend time with Tara. She would be nine that year! I thought, There might come a day when she does not want to hang out with her mama, so I wanted to spend as much time with her as I could.

Glad that the first year of college was about over, I felt all I took were useless classes. The upcoming fall semester brought classes I was really interested in: anatomy, psychology and biology. Now we were starting to get to the nitty gritty of why I went to school. I had always loved how dance made the body feel; now I was going to learn about the biomechanics and reasons why the body was able to withstand all the stresses that are placed upon it, not only by dance but by any other activity. The psychology class was mildly interesting. I learned a little about thought process and outcomes. Little did I know so much of what I would ultimately do would be related to the psyche? As far as the biology class went, it was much easier than chemistry as it was cut and dry.

The summer of 1994 quickly flew by and fall classes began. I knew now I was more than capable of handling a full credit load (18 hours), all my parental duties and home responsibilities, and I still had time to take aerobics classes and get in about 15 miles of jogging a week. I figured I could toss in a part-time job, too. I felt like I needed to contribute financially. Mark never said a word about me not working. He wanted me to focus on my studies and not worry about money. For this I was grateful, but I still felt like I had the time and energy to contribute, so I looked on the SIUE campus job-boards. Lo and behold I found a very part-time position with an education professor right here in town. He wrote manuals for teachers and he needed someone to help with book editing, formatting, marketing and administrative work. He was very passionate about his work and very good at what he did. The position actually paid well and I was able to get some experience in publishing while earning some pocket change that would help pay some of the bills. This was definitely a win-win situation.

The fall season and semester flew by, and before I knew it it was time for finals. I was very pleased with my grades and GPA - it had dipped a little, it was not a 4.0, but it was not far from it. I was not as smart as my Tara. She was always self-sufficient, eager and happy to do her homework - she enjoyed learning as much, if not more, than I. My health was good (according to my standards) and I was finally off the steroids.

The Christmas decorations went up and came down. The holidays came and went as did the family. It was a rough, snowy season, and I SOOOO hated being cold. Not to mention it is dark in the mornings and dark by 6 p.m. That was the part I hated the most. I thrive on sunshine and daylight; it's always energizing.

The 1995 spring semester at SIUE allowed me the opportunity to take an elective class. There were certainly a lot of options such as graphic design, Spanish, computer programming, NOT! I wanted to take a ballet class. I registered for a theater/dance class; I was going to take classical ballet. How exciting was this? I thought I could show these girls a thing or two. I have had a little experience you know! Well, hello, it had been 12 years since my happy ass had been in a dance studio in a leotard, tights and leg warmers while executing plies, grand jetes and pirouettes. Now, mind you, I still had my dancing attire stored away, and, yes, when I pulled them out and put them on they still fit. The sad part was my 30-year-old body didn't bend the way it once did. I thought it was going to be easier than it was! However, the dance instructor could tell I was a trained dancer who had grace, flow and technique; it was just my kicks weren't quite as high as the other students. Nonetheless, this class made me VERY SORE. A soreness I had not felt in years and I loved it! There is one thing a person can never say about a dancer is that they do not use every muscle in their body to dance, because every muscle in my body was hurting like the dickens.

I enjoyed this semester; I had a health class, an A & P (anatomy and physiology) class, a ballet class and a few other classes (that left little impression on me as I don't recall their topics). I continued with my parental and domestic duties, and work for the education professor, but the weather was so cold that going outside to run was not an option. It was actually so cold many of my classes were cancelled, not to mention Tara's school was closed as well. Come on spring! Mama wants to wear a bathing suit, not a snowsuit!

SEVENTEEN

TEN YEARS LATER

Mark and I celebrated our 10th anniversary in 1995. I couldn't believe 10 years had flown by. This was about the time we started taking vacations and long, weekend trips. One of our early travels was to Washington D.C. so Tara could be in her cousin's wedding. Even though we were only there a few days, we managed to get in as much sightseeing as we could. That year Tara and I also took a side trip to Indianapolis so I could visit with an old high school friend, and we managed to steal away a week to go to Chapel Hill, N.C. and spend time with the whole Huntley clan at Mark's aunt's lake house to celebrate their grandfather's 90th birthday. We enjoyed the lake house and we got to spend a few days in Wrightsville Beach, N.C. as well. That was until a hurricane came pounding down the coastline and we were ordered to evacuate. It is amazing to think the entire time I lived in Boca there was never a single hurricane!

Cutting our vacation to North Carolina short was OK because as soon as we got back to Edwardsville I had to get ready and organized so I could start classes in St. Louis at Fontbonne College. I was finally going to start my *real* education. I was beyond excited. I enjoyed my gen-ed studies at SIUE but those were all my have-to classes. Now, I'm enrolled and going to be taking the want-to classes. The only part about this next step I wasn't going to like was the commute. I hated traffic and I hated waiting in traffic. Not to mention, I drove a five-speed Honda and I remember my left leg going numb because I had to engage the clutch for so long as I crept across the bridge. Well, if that was the worst of it, I'll take it.

I had mostly science classes and labs for my first semester. My schedule actually was not too bad and I only had to commute three times a week. That was a good thing, but I wanted to get as much experience in the field as I could and the only way to do this was to get a part-time job in the field, so I found and applied for a job at St. Louis University (SLU) working in their food service department. They were able to work around my school schedule so my hours could be completed right after school, eliminating an additional commute. That was good and bad; good, because I would miss rush-hour traffic, but bad because my home duties were going to suffer.

The field of dietetics during the mid-'90s was a clinically driven field. Dietitians worked in hospitals, in food service, in long-term care or in the area of research. Since I was not sure what area was for me, I wanted to try them all. The job at SLU was my introduction to food service and I quickly learned I didn't want any part of this! But, I needed the experience. It would look good on my dietetic internship application and the best part was I got paid. At the point, the additional income was welcomed.

Classes were very small at Fontbonne compared to SIUE. For example, my English 101 class at SIUE had over 170 students; my chemistry class at Fontbonne had 12 students. Wow. The advantage to smaller classes was the professor knew everyone's name. I quickly made friends with everyone in the department because there were only about 55 students going through the program at that time, so it was great to get to know a little bit about everyone and a lot about others.

EIGHTEEN

THE CLASSES THAT MATTERED

I had a giant epiphany during my first semester at Fontbonne. Remember how over the course of the last few years I took aerobic classes and ran? Well, that was about to pay off. Since I lived across the river and had to commute, I needed to find a way to kill some down time between classes. Once my homework was completed and I had some free time, the first place I looked for was a fitness center. Well, Fontbonne had a Recreation Center with two huge basketball courts and a few training rooms for the wrestlers. But, there weren't any kind of aerobic or fitness rooms, and they certainly didn't offer any aerobic classes. Really! How is that possible? Why doesn't this college have a decent fitness program?

One day I approached the rec center coordinator and asked why there was not any kind of fitness program. He responded by saying they hadn't ever had any request for one. Well, dude, I'm requesting one. We talked about what types of classes other colleges were offering and what I thought the students might like. He was totally open to the idea of offering some type of class; it was just a matter of figuring out where to do it.

Being an aerobic participant is not the same as being an aerobics instructor, and an instructor should be certified. I honestly didn't know there were so many kinds of certifications available. While I was not certified, I was allowed to teach. With my dance background I did know enough about class design and I knew how to stay with the beat of the music. Plus I had taken enough classes to know the music needed to be upbeat and the instructor had to be motivating. If it was not fun, people weren't going to come back. So, the coordinator and I discussed offering a few classes to see how well they were received and the department would then decide if a fitness program would or should be something they needed to offer.

During the late 1990s, Step Aerobics was the big thing (surely one remembers Denise Austin, Jane Fonda and the introduction of the Reebok Step). There was also the TaeBo kickboxing trend and the surge of "do-it-at-home" workouts plus Hi-Low impact aerobic classes. The option to purchase equipment didn't exist, so it was decided I would teach a Hi-Low impact aerobic class. Little did I know what an impact teaching these classes would have on my future?

We started out by offering two classes. During the first few weeks there were just a few attendees, but as the word spread classes grew to 20-plus participants, which meant we were going to add classes! Yeah! This was working. The students loved it, and the athletic coaches actually had some of their players attend. I was so thrilled the classes were well received. I didn't care I was not getting paid! My payment (unbeknownst to me) was the experience!

Somehow I kept adding more and more to my plate. Now I was not only commuting, taking my academic classes and labs, teaching aerobic classes during the lunch hour, going to work at the hospital after classes - I was also fulfilling my domestic and parental duties, and I was still putting in some part-time hours with the education professor. Even though I had so much going on, I still wanted to be a big part of Tara's school experience, so any fundraiser, field trip or classroom party I could attend, I did. Thank goodness that my health was holding up. I was a little overwhelmed, but nothing I couldn't handle. The semester ended, my grades were great. Tara's grades were great. Mark was happy at the nursery and life was good. I couldn't wait until the next semester as it only brought more difficult classes I knew I would love.

The 1995 Christmas season was uneventful. Daddy came to visit, and I relaxed and enjoyed watching football as usual. I knew I needed some down time as the spring semester at Fontbonne was going to get very challenging. I had a few science classes and labs, and we were going to be taking a lot of field trips to different facilities so we could get a feel for what other dietitians did in the field. Thus allowing us the opportunity to determine if that area of dietetics was an area we wanted to pursue. Like I said before, my job at SLU allowed me the opportunity to check food service off the list, and even though I hadn't officially done any research, I knew working in a lab was not for me. This left clinical work and long-term care, and honestly neither one sounded interesting. I was looking forward to our field trips so I could get a better feel for these two areas of dietetics.

I was juggling a lot of things during the spring semester, but I plugged along and did what I had to do. By March, my arthritis was starting to give me some troubles, and by this I mean joint pain: inability to bend my elbows, stiffness in my ankles, and redness and swelling in my hands and ankles. Not sure if it was related to the cold weather or the fact my plate was full. Arthritis is one of the symptoms of Crohn's that tends to flare when your body is trying to fight off inflammation or infections. Joint aches and pains for me, as I began to learn, was usually a sign I needed to slow down. *Hmm, where could I cut back?* I had to do the schoolwork, homework and housework. I suppose I could cut back on my hours at the hospital. I could cancel some aerobic classes, ease up on the running and I suppose I could tell the professor I needed a break. But, I liked doing all these things. I totally enjoyed teaching aerobics and running was my stress relief. I know I needed the hospital work experience if I ever wanted to be accepted into a dietetic internship. The housework, laundry, cleaning, grocery shopping, bill paying, etc., was not going to do itself. Where in the hell was I going to cut back? Please don't think Mark and Tara didn't pitch in because they did, but it was my own inability to let things be less than perfect that got me in trouble.

Life is funny that way, because when people don't cut back, the FORCES OF NATURE do it for them. This very thing happened when my daddy got sick, and I flew to Florida to take care of him. The entire month of March (snack dab in the middle of the Spring semester) he was in and out of the hospital. Daddy was

84 at the time. He didn't really act 84, though he did kind of look it (sorry, Daddy!). He was a true Italian through and through. He always dressed to the nine's even if he didn't have anywhere to go. He was a very proud man with a strong belief in religion. He seemed to be doing so well living on his own; it had been four years since Mom died. He had his friends and neighbors, and he loved to work in the yard and loved to watch football. Daddy was a strong-willed and hard-headed Italian. We often would go round and round, and butt heads on many things, neither one of us backing down and neither one of us giving in: The qualities people love to hate about each other.

At the end of March, after missing four full weeks of classes I needed to get back to Edwardsville. However, I was not about to leave daddy here by himself, and he would have no part of a baby-sitter as he called it. The only other option was for him to come back to Illinois and stay with us for a while. He reluctantly agreed and off to the Midwest we went only to come home just in time for spring break. Actually, that was a blessing in disguise because it gave us (me) time to get Daddy settled in and into a new routine.

Just as I was trying to figure out how to ease back on my schedule, it got harder, and I had four weeks of homework to catch up on (not to mention tests, presentations and labs). Thank goodness all my professors were understanding and allowed me extra make-up time. It is always hard when a semester is only 12-weeks long and one misses a third of it. Not to mention I was missing one of the classes I so looked forward to taking.

It was a communications class and there were only eight of us in that class. If memory serves me correctly, it was called interpersonal communications and out of all the classes I took it was that class that was the most pivotal and had the greatest impact on me. At the time, I had NO idea the area of dietetics I would ultimately end up working in was not really dependent entirely upon my knowledge of disease, disease process and disease management, but on my ability to communicate with my clients.

This class was structured on communicating effectively with others and all our assignments were oral presentations. I decided to explore the best way for me to communicate to my classmates and professor. I tried reading verbatim from index cards; reading bullet points from index cards; reading verbatim from an overhead projector; reading verbatim from bullet points on a projector; memorization of materials; and finally, what I like to call winging it. Each time we had to present an assignment I tried a different technique. It didn't take long before I realized I was not a read it from an index card type of gal. I did better with the projector method, but often found myself veering from the bullet points and that was distracting not only for me, but for my audience. It was easy to memorize something and regurgitate it, but there never seemed to be any feeling or enthusiasm in that type of presentation, especially if the presenter got distracted, and couldn't remember where they were. My last method - the wing-it method - became the approach I took, and I found this to be my best form of communication. This method allowed me to be more passionate about the material I was conveying; to look my audience in the eye and address questions asked by the audience without feeling like I had lost my place. It also gave me the freedom to move around and interact with the audience.

Communicating in this way was a lot like dancing. It is a way to express how one feels about a subject and be passionate about the information being presented. It allows individuals to put their own flair and style into their performance. I liked it. I liked being in front of a group and sharing information with others, and I liked when everyone was watching me and was interested in what I had to say. This was truly the best class ever! Now that I look back it was the class that helped me become what and who I am today.

Obviously, I didn't enjoy all my classes this much so the makeup work in the other classes was harder.

Nonetheless, I still had to do it. I also had to get daddy established with the doctors here so he could get the injections and the treatments he needed. This actually turned out not to be so hard and we were able to find great doctors who took good care of him. Well, most of them did.

All this made me think back to my first few classes at SIUE when I would overhear the 18- and 19-year-olds talking about how many responsibilities they had and how hard it was to manage everything. Give me a flippin' break! Walk in my shoes for a few days!

Daddy never asked for anything while he stayed with us. He waited until Tara or I got home. The hardest part was he never wanted to worry me so he neglected to tell me when he didn't feel good and about the two times he had fallen down! *Really, Daddy?* I needed to know these things! Realizing he needed to regain some strength, he did agree to have a physical therapist come to the house two times a week to help him with some range-of-motion activities and exercises, and for that I was thankful. Hearing from someone else he needed to move more and eat more was a blessing. *What the heck did I know?* It isn't like I was going to school to learn all about this or anything.

The remainder of the spring semester was catch-up time for me, and I did my very best to get all my papers and presentations finished on time. It was the least I could do since all the professors were so lenient. But, it seems that just as life was getting better, my health was getting worse because my follow-up appointment with my GI doctor in May didn't go so well. He basically told me to get it together! *Yeah, yeah, yeah, I will! I promise!* Less stress? *OK, I'll work on that!* Well, it was a good thing the semester was almost over. I know I still had to get through finals, but once I jumped that hurdle, I could rest. At least, I thought I could.

Daddy had been here two full months and he felt he was strong enough to go back to Florida. I didn't think so, but I didn't have the time or energy to butt heads with him so we got him a plane ticket and he returned to Boca the end of May. He was not home for more than a few weeks before we all realized that living alone was no longer an option. And, it took time for that hardheaded Italian to figure it out for himself.

After long and careful consideration, it was decided we were going to sell my childhood home in Boca, and he would come live with us in Edwardsville. Wow, this was the only house I really knew! This was the house I grew up in! Hmm, not sure I liked this idea, but this was not about me it was about my daddy.

NINETEEN

THE END OF AN ERA

Before I could leave for Florida, I had to make sure I had all my classes in check for the Fall semester, because believe it or not I was going to graduate in December! Where in the hell did the time go? Graduation? Already? Along with the senior semester came a senior project, which required meetings, planning and presentations. Not to mention I had to begin the application process for a dietetic internship. I had three local choices: BJC (Barnes, Jewish, Christian Hospital), SLU (St. Louis University), and the VA Hospital (Veterans Administration). They only took six to 14 interns, so one had to have an amazing GPA, outstanding community service and/or lots of work experience. Well hells bells, could I just audition for the position vs. filling out an application? I can ace an audition; an application was another story. This was going to be yet another hurdle to get through.

First things first: I had to get Daddy squared away. During the months of June and July in 1996, I went to Florida. First, we had to put the house on the market (didn't know jack about real estate); have an estate sale (really, can't Goodwill just come take some of this stuff away?); and pack over 30 years worth of memories. Then, hire a moving van, close out all banking and other accounts, not to mention I wanted to make sure daddy had some together time with his friends, neighbors and, of course, our family. This was a tall order to fill in a short time.

As good fortune would have it, once our neighbors found out we were going to put the house up for sale, they expressed their interest in buying it. Praise the Lord for small favors. They had three grown children and their only daughter was newly married, and looking for a home. What better place than this? Right next door! This arrangement made me feel so relieved because I knew they would take good care of the house I grew up in. The burden of finding a realtor and listing the house was eliminated. We were also able to negotiate leaving a lot of the furnishings in the house. Just like Mark and I, we didn't have a lot of things when we first got married: the more we left, the better. This also meant no estate sale and less to move across the country. Besides, Mom and Daddy's taste in furniture and home décor (sorry guys) was nothing like mine, so there really was not a lot I wanted or that had significant sentimental value to me. OK, this was getting easier. Closing all the financial accounts didn't take too long and changing addresses was a simple process as well. This allowed me the opportunity to take Daddy around to see friends and family. Wow, something going according to plan!

By the beginning of July, Tara flew down to join me and we spent some time doing some touristy things, and going to the beach. I thought this was the last time in awhile I would be there, so I wanted to soak up as much sun as I could.

Because we were fortunate to be able to leave a lot of items behind, all I needed to rent was a larger U-haul. Mark and his brother flew down mid-July and spent a few days hanging out with friends and family, and then he and his brother strategically packed the U-haul with what was left of Daddy's worldly possessions. There was not one ounce of space left in that U-Haul by the time he was finished packing it, and on July 12th Mark pulled out of the driveway for what would be the very last time and began the drive back to Edwardsville. Daddy, Tara and I stayed one more night and headed for the airport the next morning.

I'm not sure if I cried or was relieved to be moving on, but it was a very long and happy chapter in my life that came to a close. That was the house I saw my first ghost; the house I had my first sleepover; and the house that held all my childhood memories. Oh well, it was just a house; I will always have the memories!

TWENTY

MOVING ON TO MY LAST SEMESTER

The next few weeks were spent unpacking, organizing and getting Daddy settled in. I wanted him to feel like he had his own area and space, and he needed to know where everything was in the house. Susie homemaker, I became.

August brought the beginning of school for Tara and I. Tara would be attending a school in Glen Carbon, which meant she either needed to get on the bus at the butt crack of dawn, or I had to take her. As our home was so far away, she would be the first one on the bus and the last one off, which meant my eight (almost nine-year-old) would have a 10-hour day. Not on my watch, she was not. I arranged my schedule so I was able to take her to school and Mark was usually able to pick her up or we carpooled with the other parents who lived on our end of town.

Now, my schedule consisted of my final semester of college, homework, senior preparation and presentation, hospital work, applying for internships, domestic duties, taking Daddy to the doctors, teaching aerobics, running and attempting to sleep. The added surprise was that this time when my Crohn's decided to flare, it happened overnight. I didn't have any warning; I didn't have the fatigue and lethargy; and I didn't have any abdominal pains. It was as though a light switch was turned on: I went to sleep feeling OK and woke up with severe pain AND nausea AND vomiting. *Well, isn't this special?* I don't have time for this shit! Not now! But, as the saying goes: "If one doesn't make time for health, they will make time for illness." I needed to get it together. I needed to start taking all the information I was learning about diet and disease, and put it to use on myself. How can I possibly be a role model for others if I don't walk the walk? I needed to slow down and stop burning the candle on both ends. I needed to find that gray area, you know, moderation. I ended up missing only a few days of school and work, and my doctors put me back on some heavy-duty medication, and I felt better immediately.

I could now get through my last semester. All my papers, projects and senior presentation went off without a hitch. I couldn't believe it. In a few short days, I would be walking down the aisle to accept my diploma. Wow, what a ride this had been! Graduation date: December 1997!

To summarize my non-traditional college years: Gen-ed classes at SIUE with the opportunity to revisit my dancing; commuting to St. Louis to educate myself about how diet and disease affected one's health; learning that I needed to use said principals on myself; learning to manage my time effectively; and, most importantly, to meet and become friends with those who would have a greater impact on me than they knew.

I failed to mention earlier one of the gals I became good friends with (and I am still friends with today) had a major impact on my future career choices. Remember when I said I had no idea that teaching aerobics required certifications? Well, this friend had a few certifications and one was as a personal trainer. A personal trainer - what was that? Well, it is someone who helps individuals achieve goals they have set for themselves. It is someone who takes into consideration their client's strengths, weaknesses, illnesses, physical limitations and health history, so they can design a program to help that person reach their goal(s). If I decided this was something I wanted to pursue, where does one offer this type of service?

Come to find out a certified personal trainer worked in gyms, health clubs and fitness centers, and some trainers make home visits. I liked this. It was much more specific than teaching a group aerobic class.

I very much enjoyed teaching aerobic classes and was more than thrilled when Fontbonne continued with the fitness program for their students after I left. That spoke volumes to me! They found other instructors to carry on with the classes and I was so very proud I was instrumental with the inception of this program. Teaching aerobics was also a way to make some easy extra income and the fact it was fun, and I was good at it, was even better. I knew that I needed to become certified by a reputable organization to be respected in the field and come to find out that was easy enough to do. But, the thought of becoming a personal trainer was even more exciting. My friend was certified through the American Council on Exercise (ACE). I checked out this organization first. There were a few different certifications available and I chose the Certified Personal Trainer option. This meant I purchased my study guides, materials, practice exams and then sign up for the exam. As good luck would have it the next exam was in February 1998 (a month or two away) and right here in St. Louis. I registered, paid my fees, received my huge, and heavy, textbook and began studying. This was going to be simple: the anatomy I knew, the biomechanics I knew, the class design I knew. The only parts I didn't have any frame of reference for was the business portion. But that was OK - that would be easy to learn. I studied and practiced because there was going to be a practical portion as well as a written portion.

Testing day finally arrived. I was actually quite taken aback by the close to 200 people sitting in the seats waiting to take the exam. Were all these people going to be my competition? I better ace this ACE test! The written portion was long and the questions were randomized. This test was still in paper and pencil format so every single question had to answered, and (no joke) it took about three hours to complete. Once the written portion was completed, everyone was allowed to leave for lunch and return at 1 p.m. to demonstrate the practical portion. All I had to do was go through the motions: I had been teaching classes for a while now. This was not rocket science to me! Sure enough it was my turn; I did my thing, aced my test – got my temporary certificate and was ready to rock and roll. Now, I would be able to supplement my income while I was completing my internship - I seemed to have the best of both worlds.

TWENTY-ONE

SCHOOL DOESN'T TEACH WHAT YOU NEED TO KNOW: MY MOST BENEFICIAL LEARNING

Like I said before, I didn't have the option to relocate. I had to apply for local internships. I filled out the ridiculous number of pages they all required; obtained the necessary transcripts; sealed everything in an envelope; kissed the envelope and dropped them in the mail. All I could do at this point was hope and pray I had done enough.

As luck would have it, I was accepted into the VA program. This was the next step toward reaching my goal. I couldn't have been happier and Mark and my family were so very proud of me. The up side was I was one step closer: the down side was it was an intense program that was equivalent to a full-time job.

The VA dietetic internship program consisted of class work and floor work. We had more than 12 different rotations which meant we spent time in the oncology unit, diabetes center, intensive care unit, renal/dialysis center, cardiac care unit, long-term care, community clinic, home-health and food service areas just to name a few. The program was structured so we spent one, two or even three weeks in each area depending on how intense the rotation. On each rotation, we were mentored by the dietitian who worked in that area, and as expected, we had homework, case studies, projects and presentations to complete. The internship also allowed time for us to experience the pharmacology, research and teaching opportunities that were available. Basically, an internship gave interns a snippet into each area of dietetics.

I was very excited for the program to begin, but there was not much down time between graduation and work. The VA hospital had two locations: one in downtown St Louis - their acute (surgery, dialysis, diabetes clinics, etc.) facility; and one in South County - their long-term (geriatrics, psychophrenic ward, PTSD, and kitchen) facility. The internship would require we divide our time equally between these two facilities.

During the initial orientation, we completed any remaining paperwork, received our assignments and were given our badges. The rest of our introductory week was spent touring both facilities and going through the outline for the next nine months of rotations. Just like college, there was no guesswork. Everyone knew exactly what was expected of them. The rotations were staggered amongst the six gals in our group. Once I read through the program, I quickly began mapping out my life. I made a silent commitment to myself that no matter which rotation I was in I was going to make it a point to be *like* those patients. By this I mean if I was in the diabetic clinic, I wanted to experience life as a diabetic. I followed the type of diets they were instructed to follow and I checked my blood sugars three times a day. If I was in the renal (kidney) center, I tried to follow a renal diet and monitor my fluid intake and my intake of potassium, sodium, zinc and vitamin K. If I was in the oncology ward, I made sure I drank high-calorie supplements and forced myself to lie in bed (on a weekend day that allowed me to do that) because most cancer patients have little to no energy. If it was at all possible I tried to experience what the patient did. How was I, as a dietitian, supposed to expect patients to follow all the rules, diets and suggestions I gave them if I didn't try to walk in their shoes?

Even though there were only six girls in our program, we all got along and were all very eager to learn, we were a very diverse group. Sometimes our

Monday classroom time was the only day we saw each other, because we went through the various rotations at different times. We often got together with the other two local internship groups and listened to speakers or presentations by various health departments, organizations or other dietitians in the area.

I enjoyed going to work everyday. I enjoyed learning about what really went on in a hospital. I enjoyed being able to say, "Well there is an area of dietetics I never want to practice." It was easy for me to figure out that the food service, long-term care, oncology, geriatric, pediatric and research were definitely areas I had zero interest in pursuing. It was very hard to watch how some people suffered and to see the little ones who were disabled or born with genetic disorders or the veterans who had serious mental issues and/or amputations deal with life on a daily basis. Even though, I myself was dealing with a disease on a daily basis, I should count my blessings because I felt I was much better off than these patients. I was humbled by their stories and by their strength. It further reinforced my NO EXCUSES attitude.

It's not without reason that patients don't listen to a dietitian's instructions when they are being discharged; all the patient wants is to go home. They aren't interested in hearing someone tell them they need to buy skim milk or limit their intake of red meat, or avoid sodium. Heck, I wouldn't listen to me either.

As I went through my rotations I found a few areas that were of interest to me: I enjoyed community health, home health and the cardiac/diabetic sections. During our community rotations we got to go to schools, community centers, health fairs and give presentations or set up tables with handouts and informational materials. This meant the people who were coming to you had an interest in the information available, unlike the hospital where the dietitian was told to visit a patient to provide said information. I loved my home-health rotation because I got to go into the patient's home and see what their home life, resources and support system were like. This made all the difference in the world as to the type of educational information I provided, but I won't lie - I was a little nervous about some of the areas and neighborhoods we were sent to visit a patient. Sometimes you would see bars on the windows, abandoned cars and people sleeping on the street. But, I have never felt like a scaredy cat and always felt I could handle myself. Although the territory was concerning, I liked the fact that the dietitian was able to work at one's own pace and I didn't have to go into the hospital for anything but supplies and or teaching materials. The last areas that interested me were the cardiac and diabetic units. Even though there are some unmodifiable factors (age, gender, family history) that are out of a person's control, there were many modifiable factors (smoking, exercise, diet) these patients could learn to change that would improve their health while reducing their symptoms and possibly reducing their medications. I quickly learned I liked the rotations that involved the most personal interaction, flexibility and opportunity to educate the patient.

During my internship I realized I had to let a few of my many home/fun responsibilities slide. I relinquished most household chores and duties to Tara and Mark; I quit my part-time job with the education professor; I was not teaching any aerobic classes; and I eased up on my running. My time was spent working, taking care of daddy and myself, and doing homework. The nice thing was I did receive a stipend so at least I had some gas money with a little left over to occasionally buy Tara or myself something pretty.

Good thing I had freed up some time, because daddy was not getting any younger - as a matter of fact he was actually getting really sick. He did have heart disease and had some interventions years and years ago. He had fallen a few times - and he was not the best eater either (and it was not because of my bad cooking!). He had gone through injections for prostate cancer; he really didn't like the cold; and let's face it - he was just old (87 to be exact).

Obviously, I took Daddy to all his appointments, and I usually went into the exam room with him so I was able to hear what the docs had to say. There was one visit in particular I will never forget (remember earlier when I said we had found daddy MOSTLY good doctors)? Daddy had lost weight. He and I would go round and round about him eating more. He refused, I got mad, we butted heads, and life went on. I certainly can't force a stubborn and hardheaded 87-year-old Italian to eat, especially since I was gone all day. All I could do was have his food prepared and ready in the fridge so all he had to do was pull it out and eat it. After the doctor had finished talking to Daddy, he asked to see me outside the room. He then had the balls to tell me I needed to do a better job of taking care of my father. He was too thin and weak. I thought, *seriously, dude? You didn't just say that to me! Do you have any idea of how much attention and care, and love I give my daddy?* Needless to say, this was the last time we went to this doctor!!!

A few months passed and daddy had fallen yet again. This time he broke his hip! Oh boy, now what to do? Daddy was a WWII veteran so I was able to take him to the VA hospital where I was doing my internship, and he had surgery to repair his fractured bone. Surgeries were done at the downtown center, and luckily, I was doing my rotations there. When I finished my internship responsibilities I would go up to daddy's room, eat dinner with him, watch a little TV, and then head home when visiting hours were over. He spent about seven to 10 days there, and protocol was for him to go to the South County facility for rehabilitation. Good deal because my rotation location was getting ready to change. So again this worked out very well. I would complete my rotation, eat, watch TV and then stay until they kicked me out. Daddy spent about 14 to 21 days in the hospital recovering. Upon discharge he was required to have the home-health and physical-rehab nurses come to the house to help him continue to regain his strength.

With Daddy back home and eating better, and gaining weight, I could breathe a little easier. I was already about half way through the internship and it was summer time. This year, however, I didn't get to take Tara to the pool and we didn't get to go on little mom/daughter adventures, but we enjoyed our weekends together. I had too many projects and presentations to prep for, not to mention at the end of the internship we sat for the national boards! This was a standard paper and pencil test, and took about three to four hours to complete. Intimidating to say the least! As luck would have it the pencil and paper version was coming to an end in April of 1998, so our December graduating class would be the guinea pigs that get to take the first computerized test version. Honestly, that part didn't scare me. What scared me most about the computerized test was one had to answer the question that popped up before they could move onto the next question. The problem with this was one couldn't look back or forward at any other questions. Now, I'm not sure about others test takers, but being able to look back or ahead at other questions often helped me figure out an answer if I was not 100 percent sure. Finally, this test was weighted, which meant once one got to a certain point of correct (or incorrect) answers the test just ended, so they never knew when the test would abruptly stop. The only bonus I could see was the results were given right away and one didn't have to wait for the paper and pencil score sheets to be tabulated.

It was late fall and Daddy was sick again, and this time it was his heart. He was admitted back to the downtown center (which as luck would have it, I was on rotation there). After the docs got daddy's labs, blood pressure and heart rhythm under control he was transferred to the other facility, and again as luck would have it my rotation switched as well. We repeated what we had done before. I worked, ate dinner with Daddy and left when visiting hours were over. Daddy seemed to be getting better, but it didn't seem like he was ever going to be well enough to come home. He spent quite a few months there - they treated him well, fed him well and made sure he received all the exercise and patient interaction he needed. My rotations switched between both facilities, and I visited Daddy everyday no matter which facility I was doing my rotation.

It was now December 1998, time to put up the decorations, tree, lights, shop, bake, wrap presents, and attend parties. I think this was the first year there was so much going on I did not put up a Christmas tree. It seemed I was the only one doing the work, and I didn't have the time or energy to lug a fake, boxed, 8-foot plastic tree from the attic and down the stairs. Then assemble it, drape it with lights and ornaments, etc., only to tear it all down in a few weeks, box it back up and lug it back upstairs. Tara and Mark didn't seem to want to help with the decorations that year and with daddy in long-term care I didn't feel the need to go all out, so guess what? I didn't! I thought, "Why in the heck stress myself out over this? A tree doesn't make or break Christmas! It is all about the people, being thankful and giving, right?"

It was December 23 - two days before Christmas: I had a few days off from the VA and was enjoying the break. That ended quickly when our home phone rang that night at 11 p.m. We all know it is NEVER a good thing when the phone rings that late at night! Sure enough it was the VA hospital calling to say that Daddy had died in his sleep. I knew he was not doing well, and I knew he didn't have any quality of life, but really daddy - two days before Christmas? Mark and I got in the car, and drove down to the hospital so I could give him some kisses and a final giant hug. To make matters worse, Mark's granny died a few days earlier. I'm all about remembering holidays and happy times, but I didn't want to remember a Christmas like this one.

TWENTY-TWO

FINALLY, I GET TO DO WHAT I HAVE WORKED FOR

The summer of 1999 brought the internship program to a close, and I was excited, well, rather scared, to begin my career. All the years of learning and prepping were coming to fruition. I would now be able to take all this information and start doing what I wanted to do - help people.

There were still a few hurdles to overcome, such as the national boards! Like I said before I was one of the first to take the computerized version. I ordered the materials and practice tests so I could begin studying, as I had to wait until December to take the test. That was bad and good. Bad because all the information was fresh in my head, but good because it gave me the chance to let all the material soak in and reread my school notes and study guides.

I also had the luxury to enjoy a few months of downtime. For the last four years, I did nothing but go to school, work multiple jobs, teach aerobics, fight my illness and take care of Daddy and my family. NOW I had a few months to take care of me! Wow, this was new territory! What would I do with my time if I didn't have a deadline, paper due or class to teach or take? Hmm, not sure I was going to like this. But, as fate would have it, I was able to relax and enjoy my newfound freedom. This time allowed me a chance to really think about the exam and what I wanted to do with my degree. How did I want to help people? Did I want to help those who are seriously and acutely ill? Did I want to work with those in remission? Did I want to work with those who were post-op, or did I want to take a preventative approach and work with those who wanted to lead a healthier life? I wanted to make my encounters with people as effective as possible. I wanted to be able to give people the best information possible; I wanted people to want to be healthy because being sick is no picnic and if there was a way for people to maintain their good health, then I wanted to help them stay there. However, what I have learned throughout the years is that peoples' health usually doesn't become important until something happens to them or someone near and dear to them. I knew I had my work cut out for me regardless of which path I chose to take.

It was crystal clear my mission and vision was to help people - and being the independent, let-no- grass grow under my feet kind of gal - I was sure I knew what was going to work best for me. Thoughts of owning my own business were intriguing. I could set my own hours and I wouldn't have to answer to anyone but myself. Wow that would really be a giant leap right out of school and an internship. I knew my stuff, but I needed to get some real experience before I jumped into becoming an entrepreneur and opening my own private practice.

While studying for my exam I searched the employment ads, and I quickly learned what I was qualified for. Remember, I said I would like to get a job in the home-health field; well, I couldn't do that without first having clinical experience, which didn't make sense. But, after a dietitian friend explained it to me - I realized why. Working alone in the home-health field meant you didn't have other dietitians to ask questions to or bounce ideas off of. So, a new dietitian who isn't familiar with the field might not know the right thing to do and could potentially make an error and that could have serious consequences.

I had to change my search and look for a clinical position, which typically means a hospital job - YUK! And of course, as luck would have it, there was a position available at Belleville Memorial Hospital (BMH). I realized I hadn't taken the boards, but I figured it wouldn't hurt to apply. This actually helped me buckle down with my studying because if there was a position available and I didn't pass the test, and I missed my opportunity to work clinically, I would be very mad and disappointed in myself.

The time came for me to register for the test. I paid my fees and scheduled my appointment. I remember driving to the testing facility all nervous and panicky. This was the test of all tests! After I checked in, I was led down a hallway into a glass cubicle with one lonely computer and a chair. The worker instructed me on how to log into the system and how to maneuver through the test. I was now free to begin. Honestly, this was worse than any audition or performance I ever did. I never remember being as nervous on stage as I was sitting here in front of this computer. Wow has my life changed over the years. Well, here it goes! As each question popped up I freaked out because there was a database of thousands of questions to choose from (i.e. clinical, research, administrative, business) so one didn't know what kind of question would pop up next. I knew I needed to answer 175 questions correctly - but remember this test was weighted, so if I kept getting more questions that meant I had gotten some questions wrong.

Here came and went question 175, 190, 200, 210, 213 and then BAM, the screen pops up with the message "We are tallying your score." Holy shit, what the hell! I jumped, gasped for air and froze. Does that mean I passed? Does that mean I failed? Crap, now I must just sit here listening to my heart beating in my ears, staring at the screen with my mouth hanging wide open waiting and waiting, like the song they play during the last question on Jeopardy. Finally, the screen flashes You Passed!. I wanted to yell and jump up and down, but figured the testing facility monitors might think I had lost my mind, so I celebrated quietly in my head and did a little chair dance. I printed off my score sheet to bring to the front desk attendant. Proof! I had proof I passed. *Hooray, Yippee, Yee-haa! I did it!!* I'm pretty sure when I walked out of the center I jumped up and down a few times, and did a little jig as I walked to my car. I couldn't wait to call Mark and tell him the fantastic news!

One of the first things I did when I got home was to see if the position at BMH was still available. If it was, did they still have my application and could I set up a time to interview for the position? The job was still available. I called and left a message with the chief clinical dietitian that I would like to interview for the position. I had never really interviewed for a position like this before and was not sure what to expect. Interviews and auditions are completely different. I am not showcasing my talents, I am conveying my knowledge and explaining what an asset I could be to the team. I had a few days to ponder and think about how I wanted to handle the interview. As I drove to the hospital, a variety of scenarios played out in my head and I was just making myself a nervous wreck!

I parked my car and found my way through the basement hallways to the dietitians' office. I was so nervous as I lifted my arm to knock on the office door. I entered to find two dietitians working at their desks. The chief dietitian introduced herself and I remember walking to the conference room next-door and sitting down with this woman who could ultimately be my boss. We exchanged some pleasantries and she looked over my application as she began asking me a variety of scenario questions. I was rather intimidated, but I did my best to answer honestly and quickly but not TOO quickly. She jotted a few things down on my application. She didn't have a lot of eye-to-eye contact and she didn't give off any warm fuzzies. Regardless, I answered all her questions and was on my best professional behavior. She seemed pleased with my responses and then suggested we take a tour of the hospital. We returned to the office and I met some of the other dietitians. In all, there were five dietitians employed at BMH. One worked in the long-term care center, one on the OB-GYN floor, one on the cardiac floor, one on the ICU and IMCU units, and the last dietitian covered the remaining patient load. BMH also employed a part-time, outpatient dietitian who worked in the office just a couple days a week. Each dietitian was ultimately responsible only for their floors, but if the hospital was at full capacity or there were more consultations than a dietitian could handle, the gals would help each other out. So each dietitian really needed to know a little about each unit and become familiar with all the doctors and head nurses on these units. This also helped when it was your turn to work the weekend shift; on weekends one had to cover the entire hospital. All the dietitians seemed very nice and I thought I would like working there, especially since I learned I would be replacing the dietitian who was working on the cardiac floor (one of the areas I loved!).

It was my great fortune that I received a call back and was offered the job. I accepted the position and was told I needed to come to the personnel department to fill out the paperwork and attend orientation. December 1999 began my dietetic career.

TWENTY-THREE

MY TIME AS A CLINICAL DIETITIAN

If a person has ever been employed by a big organization or a health facility they likely recall going through the orientation and training process. Boring! I know I need to wash my hands before leaving the restroom; I know I need to wear closed-toed shoes; I know I need to wear a lab coat; I know I can't carry around a Big Gulp; and I know I can't randomly access patient information. What I don't know is how to use the facility's antiquated computer system and why are there still paper charts? This is not 1982!

After learning all the ins and outs of the system, and finding my way around the hospital, I began to settle down. The gal I was replacing was extremely helpful. She had a great rapport with the hospital staff and knew everything there was to know about cardiac nutrition. Boy did I have some big shoes to fill, but as always, I was up for the challenge. After all the training and spending a few days with my mentor, I was on my own. I had so much to learn.

There is much more to clinical dietetics than meets the eye. One not only needs to know about the computer system to enter patient notes; they need to know how the kitchen food-system works; what supplements were available; how to enter food requests; how to, or better yet, where to leave notes for the doctors so they would see AND read them, and then hopefully sign off on them. A clinical dietitian also needs to know about meal rounds and care rounds, and staff/patient team meetings. Not to mention there were often ER consults, unexpected discharge consults, floor transfer consults and family request consults on top of the automatically generated consults if a patient met certain criteria. One was never sure what the day would bring. Some days there were four to five consults (very manageable); some days six to eight consults (challenging especially if there was education involved) and some days eight-plus consults (overwhelming). It all depended on the type of consult. It took a few months to get into the routine of knowing what to expect, which doctors made special requests and which nurses would get your recommendations honored.

I finally found my groove and was into a routine. The part I liked best about the position was patient education. Well, that is mostly true. I liked it when I had ample time to do it. I hated it when a doctor ordered a consult as the patient was being discharged and we had to see this patient before they could leave. Those patients NEVER wanted to see us, wait for us, listen to us and lord knows where they put the educational information we gave them. They usually sat at the edge of the bed, fully clothed, legs crossed, arms crossed, shaking their head like they were listening to us. As one might imagine, not very effective!

Hospitals have a very specific set of criteria they must comply with to meet state and federal health laws and regulations. We were required to use education materials that had been approved by the hospital administration. Most of the time I found this information to be outdated, mundane and boring! But I was not able to create a handout, as that would take an act of congress to get the new materials approved. I had to use the black and white, plain-Jane materials that were available (outdated and recopied so many times they were crooked on the page).

Now, when we had ample time to properly educate the patient (and often a family member, too), I felt like I was more effective. A lot of times we spoke more directly with the family member who would be taking care of them and cooking their meals. This was the ideal situation. But, ideal and reality rarely met!

I also liked (and disliked) meal rounds, but meal rounds were mandatory. We needed to be sure the patients were getting the right food and eating it, and if they were having any difficulty chewing the food. We also checked to see if the patient was consuming any nutritional supplements we may have ordered for them. That was all part of the process I didn't like. What I liked was getting a chance to sit down and talk with some of the patients.

People often assume every patient has a family, job or a busy life. But more often than not patients lived alone, were retired and often didn't leave the house. These were the people who had great stories to tell. First they were usually older than dirt, had been around long before WWII – some of them not only lived through WWII, they were WWI veterans! These are the men and women who made you cry when they talked about going off to war or watching their fellow soldiers die, or having a limb amputated. They also talked about working on the farm, milking the cows and planting, and reaping the crops. They were a proud generation who worked so very hard for what they had and are responsible for a lot of what WE have today.

I could spend hours sitting there listening to them tell their stories, but that was not an option. Instead I had to finish my meal rounds so I could go educate a patient who was not going to listen to me or better yet visit patients we used to call frequent flyers. These were the patients who were admitted every month or two. They never followed instructions, likely didn't take their medications and more than likely ate whatever they wanted. But, because of their compromised health, their admission generated a consult. This meant we had to review their chart, visit them and try once again to explain why they couldn't, or shouldn't, eat the way they were eating presently.

I clearly remember walking into a patient's room who I had seen numerous times before and asking them point blank: *"Are you going to listen to a word I am going to say this time? Because if you aren't, you are wasting my time and yours?"* This patient responded by saying they likely weren't going to follow my instructions. So I thanked them, left the room and documented in my chart note the patient had refused my information. Should I have been so blunt? Probably not. But seriously, after four, five or six times of seeing this same patient it was clear he was going to do what he wanted. My time is valuable and if there was a patient who was going to listen and maybe follow my recommendations, I wanted to spend time with them. This is one of the reasons I hated clinical dietetics. One HAD to visit patients and go through the process of chart reviews, and documentation, sometimes all for nothing. I wanted to work with the people who wanted to learn how to improve or manage their health. Man, I hated this job sometimes.

The only thing that kept me there was the fact I needed the experience AND I was asked to be a part of the hospital's community-based weight loss program. This was a 12-week nutrition program for people to attend a weekly session where we (the dietitians) would educate them on proper nutrition and healthy eating. OK, so these people wanted to be here; they signed up to be here. I liked that, but after reviewing the materials I didn't like how the program was structured. First off, 12-weeks was too long and secondly, there was a weekly weigh in that always made me feel like we were focusing on their weight and not about lifestyle change. The materials were just OK and the program didn't really address exercise unless they opted to join the health center (then they received access to the gym, but not information on how long, how intense or how often to work out). Shall I go on? OK, I will. The program didn't provide any one-on-one (or specialized) education; it didn't give a grocery store tour option; it didn't provide any follow-up classes or refresher classes after the 12-week program was over, and it didn't come with a binder to store all the information. While the concept was great, it definitely needed some revision and just like creating a new patient education handout, making or changing this program that has WORKED for years was like pulling teeth. If this program worked so well, why were the same people signing up time after time? Clearly that is a sign some component of the program is missing.

I liked the program concept, so it got me thinking, *How could I create and structure a program like this?* Did I even like the wording - weight loss - maybe it should be a health and wellness program? Regardless, I had plenty of time to work on and develop a program I thought would be effective.

It's funny when people start a new career or take a new job, or begin any new venture for that matter, they are hopeful and optimistic, eager and willing to do whatever it takes. I wanted every patient to be as eager to learn about health and disease management as I. I wanted every patient to have faith in themselves and the focus, drive and dedication it takes to make lifelong lifestyle changes. I wanted everyone to succeed! What I found out in the few years I worked clinically is very few are eager; even fewer have the confidence in themselves that they can make changes; and only a handful actually succeed.

Wow, it was like my bubble was bursting. I have all this information and knowledge to share. There is all the research to back up why this will work and how much better individuals are going to feel. What is the matter with people? Don't they get it? If they don't make any changes their quality of life is diminished, they lose time at work, they might not be able to play with their kids or grandkids, go on vacations, not to mention all the medications they might need to take. Is this really the route they choose? Are they really so unwilling to try? Are they afraid they might not succeed? Possibly even fail (again)?

I learned with my Crohn's that there was often not any warning when a flare up would happen. I learned - yes, the HARD way - I needed to take control of my health or it was going to control me. I'm not afraid of hard work; I'm not afraid to give it my all; and I'm not afraid if I didn't succeed the first time I'm doomed to failure. If life were easy, simple and could be controlled by popping pills or wearing gadgets, wouldn't everyone be healthy? Wouldn't the rate of obesity be going down, not up?

Life isn't easy; life can throw curve balls; and life challenges one's spirit, mind and determination. Life doesn't come with a manual or instructions. One has to figure it out for themselves. And if one has so little self-esteem they don't, or can't, even believe in themselves, how am I in a few minutes - sitting here in a sterile hospital room - going to make a difference in their life?

Maybe I'm too optimistic! Too energized! Too eager! Too dedicated! Maybe I set the bar way too high. I choose to believe in everyone: I always have and I always will. I think people think because I'm thin and fit I don't have any frame of reference as to what it is like to be overweight. And while this is true, it is also true they don't have any reference as to what it is like to use the restroom 10 - 15 times a day; what it is like to have excruciating pain, cramps, diarrhea, swelling in their hands and feet, fever, arthritis and fatigue for days and sometimes weeks on end. Remember we each carry our own baggage. I can't empathize with them or them with me; but I can sympathize with them. As their struggles are no less than mine, they are just different. And that is why I wanted to become a credible and licensed dietitian – so I can offer hope to anyone who is willing, ready and able to make their life different.

I was so ready to move on from this clinical position, but I needed more experience: two years total to be exact. I continued working with and educating patients to the best of my ability each and every time I had the opportunity. I did make a few suggestions about the community weight-loss program and the hospital actually expanded the program to include more exercise information and education at the health club. And I got to be the one to provide this service. Who would have thought my personal trainer's certification would come in handy this soon? This meant that during the first week of the program we added some very important parameters. I took their measurements, obtained their body composition using bioelectrical impedance, and did some cardiorespiratory and strength testing. Then as they progressed through the program they learned how and why exercises are done in a certain way to reach a certain goal. Once the program ended we remeasured and retested them to see how well they did. This added feature to the program gave participants tangible, measureable results.

My biggest epiphany during the time I was working with the weight loss/exercise program was that people like, want and need the personal touch. People like human contact. They like to have their body positioned so that they were using proper form. They like to be shown the right way to stretch, and they like the individualization. I truly believe these patients worked harder and were more dedicated than those who opted not to participate in the health club portion of the program. It was almost as though they didn't want to disappoint me. But it was me who didn't want to disappoint them - I wanted them to have all the tools and knowledge so they knew they could safely continue after the program was over.

During the training sessions at the health club, the patient and I talked about a lot of things and most were never hesitant to share their personal information and stories. Granted, sometimes it was too much information, but there must have been something about my style or personality that made them feel comfortable. This sharing of information actually helped me to better understand where their head was; where they had been; what their habits were; and what were their strengths and weaknesses. If I knew what motivated them, then I could give them the right type of workouts, materials and education to help them achieve success. One doesn't challenge a new runner to run a mile: they challenge them to run for 15 seconds. You build their confidence. Then challenge them to run for 30 seconds and so on, and so forth. Once they believe they can do it, they light up and smile, and are so very proud of themselves. That to me was what this profession was all about: finding the niche that worked for each person. Like I said before, we all carry different baggage. What works for one isn't going to work for the other!

I spent the next year dividing my time between the hospital and the health club. Man did I like it there. I liked it so much I got back into teaching aerobics. I began with a few classes after work a few nights a week. I taught Step Aerobics (which was still popular), Spinning (which was just becoming mainstream), strength training classes and other random aerobic-style classes. My one or two classes per week quickly turned into three or four and then five or six. I also had requests for a few private, personal training sessions on top of the classes, which was great.

I realized to be taken seriously I needed to obtain an aerobic certification, just like I had with my personal trainer's certification. There was one component of this profession I was never going to fudge on and that is I would spend the money to be certified, registered or licensed with a reputable organization. That way when people took my classes they knew that I knew what I was doing; knew how to modify moves to adapt to participants abilities; and knew what to do should someone get hurt or have a medical issue.

One of the few organizations at the time that certified aerobic instructors was the Aerobics and Fitness Association of America (AFAA). I registered, sent in my dues and fees, received my manual and study guide, and began preparing for the exam which not only had a written component, it had a practical component as well. That was OK. That was like me dancing in front of an audience. Aerobic instructors needed to be able to cue properly, stay with the beat of the music and challenge participants while making the classes fun and motivating. The testing time approached quickly. When the day finally arrived I was quite excited. I drove to St. Louis, signed in and was given my registration number. Just like the personal trainer exam, this exam was also structured so that one took the written test first, took a break and went back for the practical part. Nary a care - I had this one. Both portions of the exam went well and I was given my temporary certificate before I left and was told I would receive my official papers in the mail. I already had a BS in Nutrition, R.D. (registered dietitian), L.D. (licensed dietitian), and CPT (certified personal trainer) after my name. Now I could add I was a proud member of AFAA!

I immediately called the health clubs and gyms in Edwardsville. Seems they all were looking for instructors or at least subs to call on. I filled out the employment forms at three different facilities and it didn't take long before some of the girls were calling looking for me to sub. I could sub or I could pass - I liked having the flexibility to choose.

Even though work was busy for me, Mark, Tara and I were able to steal away for a long week and take another trip to Washington, D.C. There was so much to do in D.C. and in the surrounding areas a long weekend really was not enough. Not to mention I had family there and a friend from Fontbonne to visit (the one who encouraged me to get my personal trainer's certification). I wanted to be sure we had the chance to see everyone and everything, so the trip was planned down to the minute.

As 2000 was coming to an end, I was working fulltime at the hospital, teaching community health classes at the health club and teaching multiple aerobic classes in multiple places, and I also started offering a few private in-home training sessions, too. Family life was fantastic: Tara was enjoying school and Mark was busy as always with his remodeling business. My health was in tip-top shape. I couldn't be happier! Well, I could be if it was not so bloody cold outside, and if it was not the first Christmas without daddy.

TWENTY-FOUR

MOVING ON TO WHAT I WANT TO DO; NOT WHAT I HAVE TO DO

I had been at the hospital for two years. I enjoyed it most days, but I felt micromanaged and was not allowed the freedom to be creative and experimental. I slowly began looking for other opportunities. There was not much else out there that interested me. Sure, there were other clinical positions and there were opportunities in St. Louis, but nothing that jumped out at me and said, Apply! I remained where I was and plugged along. My performance reviews were always great and my rapport with the staff was stellar. I just didn't like this type of dietetics.

Since I worked on the cardiac floor, one of our surgeons asked if I would be interested in watching him perform open-heart surgery. Well, hell yes I would like to see this! Not only would I be better able to understand what the surgeons did, I would be better able to understand how and why the patients were so sore. I loved the human body; it has always amazed me and to be able to see it from the inside, well even better. The surgeon told the staff I would be joining in and to make me feel welcome.

You know the only thing I didn't like about the whole experience is that operating rooms are cold! I was told to stand at the head of the operating table; I was actually right over the patient's head looking directly down into their chest cavity. I observed all the preparations: the anesthesiologist role, watching the patient being hooked up to the by-pap machine, and closely watched what every nurse did. It was like a choreographed ballet; everyone knew his or her part. No one tried to cut in front of another; no one tried to take over someone else's role. They all just danced around each other in perfect unison.

After all the preparations were made and the patient was under, the surgeon cut into and pulled back the chest skin and muscle, exposing the rib cage. He picked up the loppers and cracked the sternum, and pulled it outward anchoring it open with giant clamps. Now that was a weird, odd and kind of gross sound. Then, there below me was this beating heart along with the lungs and other assorted vessels, arteries and veins. WOW! I was glad I was wearing a mask because I think I drooled a little! It was amazing to see!

The lungs weren't anything like I thought they would be or as they are portrayed in pictures. They are actually very small looking, flat Frisbees - kind of gray, too. But the heart, wow, that was unbelievable. To see all the vessels and blood, and muscle and fat in and around it was something to this day I can close my eyes and still visualize! The procedure lasted about two-and-a-half hours. All went well and the surgeon released the clamps holding open the ribcage; used thick wire to tie it back together; and finally sutured the patient. Now I understood why patients held pillows over their chest when they coughed and why they were so sore and bruised. It all made sense now. Of the two years I worked there, those two-and-a-half hours were the best.

Watching surgery gave me a better perspective when talking with the patients about how and why they shouldn't resume their old ways. If I could tell them what I saw and how what they ate and did, or didn't do, affected the integrity of their veins, maybe they would change their ways. This made me even more passionate about why they should change and how important it was to their health. Well, this just frustrated me even more because people just didn't see it or understand it.

I continued my search for a new position. Lo and behold I found a home-health position through

Barnes Jewish Christian Hospital (BJC). I applied (online) and got a call to come in for an interview. This was a part-time position because the dietitian received consultations on a random basis.

Remember, home-health was an area that I really enjoyed. I took a sick day and drove to the BJC St. Louis office for my interview. BJC currently had a dietitian who covered the Missouri side, but they were in need of someone to cover the Illinois side - perfect! I met with a great lady who was very friendly and explained the position as such: I would receive consultations for patients who needed follow-up nutritional care after their release from the hospital. I would have five business days to contact them and schedule my visit. I would have my own computer so I didn't have to drive to the office except for meetings, and to pick up my paycheck. So far, sign me up! I was told I would be reimbursed for mileage, but my territory was rather large. That was OK; I didn't mind at all. I just needed to go buy a map - GPS was not really that big in the cars 12 years ago, so a good old-fashioned street guide was what I needed. The remainder of the interview went very well. I was certain I would be hired; and I was. Even though it was a part-time position, I would be paid much more per visit than I was per hour at the hospital and now I had freedom to take on more aerobic classes and personal training sessions. This was turning out to be a win-win situation!

I know this might sound harsh, but nothing gave me more pleasure than giving my notice to my boss and I actually gave her four weeks notice if I remember correctly. This gave the hospital plenty of time to advertise for the position and for me to train the new employee. Regardless, my boss couldn't have made the last four weeks any more miserable than she did. Our department had one of the highest employee turnover rates. The problem was they needed to let the chief clinical dietitian go (my boss) and then more than likely the rest of us would have stayed longer. There is nothing worse than dreading going to work! My boss spent the final weeks following me around to be sure I wasn't goofing off since I was leaving. *REAL-LY, lady? I'm 34 years old! Get off my back!*

I knew I would miss the other dietitians I worked with since there are only so many dietitians in the area, but I was certain our paths would cross again. The four weeks flew by and before I knew it I was cleaning out my desk and moving on. *Adios, Ciao, Auf Wiedersehen! I'm out of here! Let's get this final exit interview over with. I have bigger fish to fry!*

The transition between positions was easy. I also started teaching aerobic classes on a permanent basis. So I knew each week what to expect and I could schedule my consultations around the classes. I also picked up a PRN (on an as needed basis) position with another hospital. I only worked there when someone went on vacation. Again, I had the option to accept or decline the request.

As with the clinical position at BMH I had to go through the same initial employee hire process at BJC. OK, I knew I had to do it! There were only two days of orientation and paperwork, and during that time I was educated on how to work the computer referral system. In addition, I learned how to chart my notes after I saw a patient. I purchased my street guide, made sure my vaccinations were up to date and I was ready.

My first referral was in May 2001 and I remember it well. It was at a home right here in town. I reviewed the chart (hospital notes, labs, nurses comments). I knew what I needed to talk with the patient about and the trunk of my car was filled with nutritional guides/handouts, and even food models. I was not nervous about going to a stranger's home: I knew this person needed help and my job was to guide them as best I could. The neat thing about home health is that while in a patient's home, one can go into their kitchen to look at what tools they had available. I usually spent no more than one hour with a patient. I provided my cell phone number and contact information should they have additional questions, and I left my instructions in the patient-care binder so any other health-care professional who came to visit knew what I had discussed. The final piece was to create my chart note in the computer and I was finished. I liked this new position. I kept detailed records of whom I saw; what I said; and how long I was there.

The referrals kept coming and I began to find myself driving 20, 30 even 45 minutes away for a visit. That was OK! What was not OK were some of the neighborhoods to which I was sent! For the love, how do some people live in such filth!

I clearly remember one mobile home down in Southern Illinois that had more yard art than a Home Depot garden store. Once I made my way to the front door, rang the bell and was let in, I found the inside of the home to be more cluttered than the front yard. There were only paths through the rooms and every room had boxes piled from floor to ceiling. I'm not joking when I say it looked like I was in an episode of "*Hoarders.*" This person could have lost a small child in that house and not known it! Anyway, I did my thing and got the heck out of there as fast as I could.

As the months passed I didn't think I could enter any place worse: wrong! There was a consult in Alton, a town about 15 minutes from Edwardsville. Alton is an older town with lots of character and many different neighborhoods. Once I arrived at the address, I actually sat in my car and considered not going in, but I didn't think I had that option. I walked up to the half-screened-in porch and walked through the beaten up storm door to the front door, knocked and then the dogs started barking. I didn't like the sound of this. I began to wonder if I was safe. The front door looked like it had 20 years of fingerprints on it, so what does the inside look like? A feeble old lady opened the door, I introduced myself and she let me in – I was immediately overcome by a nauseating stench, and the dirt and filth was unbelievable. She led me to the kitchen table and invited me to sit down; I quickly declined when I saw there were roaches crawling across the table. I thanked her and told her I would stand. I honestly felt like I was being bitten and shortly after leaving the home I had a welt pop up on my arm – GROSS – I went directly to the BJC ER and was treated for bug bites and given some antihistamines and creams. After the home office got the ER report of my visit, I learned I could decline a referral if I felt the surroundings, or I, were unsafe in any way. Good handy tidbit of information to know!

It was just amazing to me how some people's homes were complete garbage pits while others were pristine, sparkly and shiny. Yes, I saw people from every socioeconomic status. Though the majority of the people I saw couldn't afford a loaf of bread: How were they supposed to afford supplements to make them stronger?

Another consult I clearly remember was one I had in East St. Louis. This town is known for certain neighborhoods that could be very unsafe. I learned if I did these consults between 10 a.m.-1 p.m. I was safe as the drunks and the drug addicts were still passed out, and the homeless were out searching for food. I had received a consult for a patient who was on a tube feeding. There were two houses next door to each other; the patient was in a lone bed in the middle of the room of one house and the family lived next door. I assessed and instructed the family on how to change her feedings, leaving them with detailed and specific instructions. A few weeks later I received another consultation for the same patient. The first time I was there, there weren't any problems even though I was in an iffy part of town. This second consult was scheduled for a Tuesday, but I called to reschedule and a very good thing I did. I learned via Breaking News the Haz-Mat Bomb squad was at that house the day I had originally been scheduled to be there: I would have been right in the middle of gunfire. Wow, someone was certainly looking out for me! THAT made me nervous and I never got nervous! Needless to say, I declined any future consults to that address!

There was one other visit to a man who lived in the housing projects in Alton that sticks out in my mind. After my assessment, evaluation and instruction this man wanted to give me a hug for visiting him. He was kind of creepy anyway, which made me feel slightly uncomfortable. *Really dude, you think I'm going to hug you? Don't get up; I'll let myself out, thanks!*

Otherwise, all the other visits were uneventful. I enjoyed this position very much. There were a few times I needed to go into the office for in-services and a few times I had to get my computer updated, but otherwise I was free to do my thing. I felt like I was making a difference in people's lives. Except for the sad cases where the patients were really sick and were close to being placed on hospice: That was so heart-breaking. The only consolation I could see was these patients were in the comfort of their own home and with family.

I continued with BJC for the next year or so and I continued teaching aerobics, personal training and occasionally taking PRN calls at the hospital. The hardest part about my life at this time was that while I enjoyed everything I was doing, I felt like I was being pulled in 17 different directions. I worked from home; I charted at home; I created programs, nutritional handouts, newsletters, worked on my aerobic routines and personal training programs. It seemed like I was always working. I didn't have a dedicated area to work - no real desk or office chair per se - so I never felt like I put in my eight hours and went home.

In spite of all the craziness, Mark, Tara and I found time to take a few mini vacations to Chicago, San Diego and Hollywood. Getting out of dodge is such a great feeling. People forget what it is like to be spontaneous because everyone gets stuck in their routine.

The hardest part about traveling, for me, is worrying about food and what or where I will be eating. That is one area that needs to stay constant! The last thing I want is to be on a walking tour and not know where is the closest restroom. Foreign food causes quite the uproar in my gut and that is something I don't want to deal with when I'm away from home. And by uproar I don't just mean urgency – I mean gas, bloating and cramping. There is nothing more painful than having to pass gas, but you can't because of your location: Makes for a miserable rest of the day. I always take ample time before we leave to be sure I can locate a health food store or grocery store near our hotel that has the items my belly considers normal. It hasn't been uncommon for me to only subsist on the foods I bring - and not eat out at all. Not necessarily the healthiest approach, but it works. It's bad enough lugging all the medicine bottles with me, but bringing the food, too, used to take up an entire carry-on bag.

As 2003 rolled around, there is the tiny little fact that our daughter needed to start looking into colleges, which meant taking a few days off to travel and explore different campuses. She had her sights set on a few institutions in Chicago and three mid-state. She needed to be sure these were the only places that met her goals, as I/we didn't have the time and money to visit every school.

Overall my health was fair and I plugged along with my daily routine. I was beginning to pick up more personal training sessions in people's homes and the local YMCA gave me shot a offering a six-week "Healthy Weight" program. It was my very first opportunity to take what I had learned at BMH and offer my own version! The way I wrote my program was to address six topics I felt were important especially since it was the beginning of a new year. I started week one with Resolutions; week 2 - Fad Diets; week 3 - Rate Your Plate; week 4 - Label Reading; week 5 - Dashboard Dining; and we ended the program with a class called, Putting It All Together. I felt this covered a good variety of general nutrition. I loved that it was well received and there were over 15 participants who signed up for the program. I had a chance to work out some kinks and find what worked, and what didn't work: baby steps in program creation, modification and revision. All of these proved to be very helpful in the long run.

I also contacted a health club in Alton and they were excited to have me offer my program to their participants. The group there was not as large, but again, it gave me the chance to change topics, and revise the order and the length of the program. I realized the program wouldn't only be offered during the beginning of the year, so "Resolutions" might not always be the best way to start.

At this point, I was really all over the place: offering nutrition programs at two health clubs; teaching up to 15 classes a week at four different gyms; personal training clients in their home; taking home-health consults from BJC; and personal training clients at the health club in Belleville. Also, I was trying to work on building fall workshops, classes and nutritional informational sessions, which meant contacting newspapers to market my ideas to local businesses. This was making me one tired lady. Not to mention there were still the tiny little tasks of home responsibilities and just because I taught aerobic classes doesn't mean I didn't work out otherwise. I never tried to get in MY workout while trying to monitor a class full of participants: that would not be fair to them. I began to wonder if there was not a better way to provide all these services. I can't keep up this pace without crashing and burning at some point. And if history repeats itself, and I don't slow down, my Crohn's will flare and it will slow me down whether I want it to or not.

What other options were out there? How could I accomplish everything I wanted without being in two places at the same time? And moreover, shouldn't I be making more money for what I was doing? Not that what I was doing was about the money, but between membership dues, license renewals, dietetic and aerobic liability insurance, continuing education, wear and tear on my car, etc. - I needed to rethink everything. I toyed around with the idea of opening my own facility, but when you sit down and hash out all the costs involved it is downright scary. Between rent, property insurance, real-estate taxes, utilities, signage, furniture, flooring, equipment, advertising and all the other little incidentals, it almost made me cry. But, how cool would it be to actually fulfill a dream and do my own thing, and have people call and come to me for help and guidance? This was a huge, gigantic and big step, but if I didn't try it how would I know if it would work?

The other part of this equation bothering me was that the value of my knowledge didn't match my income, and I felt the only way to increase revenue was to put all this knowledge and experience together, and get my Master's degree. How in the heck was that suppose to happen? How am I going to squeeze even more work into my already crazy-busy schedule? Something would have to give: A master's program can be anywhere from 125-140 credit hours depending on whether the student is choosing the thesis or non-thesis route. This means I could be taking up to three graduate classes per semester. But with the option to take summer classes, I could complete this program in as little as 16 months.

Well, Mama's not getting any younger, so if I'm going to do this, I'm taking the fast route. Mark and I spent some time discussing my idea, as it would cost a big chunk of change for tuition, especially since Tara would be going to college in the fall. There was one option I could explore and that was to apply to be a GA (graduate assistant). That meant I TAUGHT classes while I TOOK classes and the school covers tuition costs. That would be awesome, but there are only a few GA positions available every year. It could be tough to get one. Again, I wouldn't know unless I tried and applied. LIFE WITHOUT LIMITS! Mark and I thought if I applied and got a position then it was meant to be, and if I didn't get chosen then I would have to take a class at a time and keep my day job(s).

I researched SIUE's kinesiology department options for majors and downloaded the GA application, and began filling out the forms. I actually found I had plenty of experience for the types of classes a graduate assistant would be required to teach as I have been teaching aerobics and training people for quite a few years now. The areas of interest in the kinesiology department curriculum I liked were exercise physiology and sport psychology. I liked how the body worked and I liked how the mind played a major role in how the body responded, so I wanted to master these two areas. I know the application process would take awhile, so I started filling out the paperwork right away: While I wanted to start in the fall of 2004 - a year away - I wanted to be sure I was accepted.

TWENTY-FIVE

GOOD TIMES, NOT SO GOOD TIMES

June and July 2003 flew by, but August found Mark and I taking a quick two-day trip to Boca for my 25th grade-school reunion! Yes, St. Joan of Arc had a grade school reunion and surprisingly 65 out of the 80-plus students in our class showed up. There was a party on Friday night at the best little bar in Delray Beach - Boston's. Loved this place! We took over the entire upstairs and had a blast catching up with long-lost friends and realizing we were old. But it was so much fun to see everyone. It was a whirlwind weekend, but well worth it.

Once back home, it was right back to the old routine. The next few months passed quickly and if working all the time was not enough we were taking day trips with Tara to check out colleges. The holidays came and went without incident. The year 2004 was full of new possibilities and our daughter's graduation from high school. Wow, where the heck did 18 years go? She was excited and nervous about graduating, and about heading off to college. Remember, Tara has always been a pleasing girl, she never wanted to disappoint anyone and going away was a big step. Her initial ideas to go away to a school near Chicago soon became, "I think I'll consider colleges closer to home." So after a lot of consideration, she finally decided on Eastern Illinois University (EIU) as it had a great literature and English program. She would still be away from home, but close enough should (ha-ha) she want to come home for a weekend.

March of 2004 brought about a sad time in the Huntley household. David, my father-in-law, died unexpectedly in his sleep on March 10. You just never know when it is your time. David had some health issues, but no one really thought they were life threatening. David and I had a great relationship: We would argue at times and agree at times. We would fight and we were both stubborn. I actually liked to pick fights with him. But he never let me forget about flooding his basement; or ruining the green bean casserole; or Tara's Chinese silk pajamas; or trying to make jello salad four hours before dinner.

LIFE WITHOUT LIMITS

I can't even begin to imagine how Mary Deane felt when she went downstairs to see why David hadn't come up to bed and found him *asleep* in his favorite easy chair. After so many years of marriage I think couples take so many things for granted. I know I do. You get into a daily routine that becomes drone and sometimes boring and mundane. You forget you once flew by the seat of your pants and did whatever the heck you wanted to do when you wanted to do it. You didn't have children or co-workers, or others who relied on you or needed you to be certain places at certain times. I realize we make our own choices and I guess to some degree we can be spontaneous if we want, but it seems like life's obligations usually win over. After so many years of togetherness, I can't imagine the feeling half of you is missing.

I can honestly say I still get a happy feeling when I see (or hear) Mark's truck pulling into the driveway. Even though there are things he does that drive me batty, I have never wanted to change the man I married and I'm amazed at how many women want to. WHY? Why marry a man if he isn't just like you want him to be? Do you really think they are going to change? Do you not think they won't rebel or pull away? Don't you think it will drive you crazy if they don't change? All you do is sound like a bitchy hag. Nag nag nag. I didn't marry Mark because I wanted to mold him into something he isn't; I married him because he made me laugh, made me happy, made me feel safe and protected, and yes, sometimes he made me cry. But I'm no peach to live with either and he isn't trying to change me! If there is one thing I wish for more than anything in the world it is for Tara to find a man like Mark, David or my daddy. These are good men; respectful, honest, hard-working, loving and smart.

Well – everyone came home for the funeral and since David was so instrumental in the conceptualization of the University Museum and getting the Art Department up and running at SIUE, he was very well known in the community, so the visitation was crowded to say the least. I hate these things - visitations I mean. When I die, I want a party: A celebration of the good times.

My brother-in-law gave an eloquent eulogy. I remember it being cold and rainy. I chose not to go to the gravesite and watch them lower his casket into the ground. Didn't need that visual for the rest of my life. Actually I have never been to his gravesite. As my luck would have it, he does talk to me on occasion. The cemetery where he is buried is about a half mile from our house on a busy street that leads out of town. I take this street when I head toward SIUE or the interstate, and one day as I was driving past I glanced over and said, *"Hey David how the hell you doin?"* And I got a response.…*"Still dead, ya dumbshit."* I laughed and laughed - because that is exactly how we would have talked to each other if we were talking face-to-face.

Seems David talks to his daughter quite a bit and I think Mark feels jealous because David never talks to him. The hardest part about David's death for Mark has been that he had been crazy busy at work and hadn't been to visit his dad in quite a few weeks. He kept meaning to go, but never did and then he died. I know this has weighed on him heavily and bothered him for a long time - I know he beats himself up over it. So the moral to this story is life can be cut short at any time. We are NEVER too busy to take a few minutes out of our day to call family or stop by and say Hi! That's much better than spending a lifetime regretting your decision not to go.

The spring of 2004 was otherwise uneventful. I did get laryngitis a few times and I did have a mini flare up, but nothing that stopped me or slowed me down. There were big events coming up: Tara's graduation and my 40th birthday!

Tara was so excited and yet somewhat scared. Everyone is excited to get out of high school, but once reality hits that they are now more or less adults and will have lots of responsibilities, and must manage their own time, they get a little nervous. Of course they think they want to travel and backpack through Europe, or get their own apartment or start their own business. But when you explain all the commitment, cost, time investment and energy that is involved, they kind of go, *Oh my, really?!? Yes really! Did you think it was easy?* But my girl knew she was headed off to EIU with about 12 others from her high school: She was nervous, but anxious to move on.

TWENTY-SIX

TURNING THE BIG 4-0!

As for me, my 40th birthday was right around the corner. I was not really worried about turning 40. It kind of seemed empowering! Thirty was my rough transition; going from 20-something to 30? That sucked. But 40 seemed OK for some reason. Especially since I had been chosen to be a GA at SIUE, I would start taking and teaching classes in the fall. I tried to determine which of the many jobs I had that would have to go by the wayside when I started grad school. The thing was that each job was so flexible I could do it whenever I wanted, but I would now have to use that flexible time for homework and projects, and thesis writing. Yes, I chose the thesis route just in case — someday — I decided I wanted to have PH.D. after my name (everyone says it stands for piled higher and deeper). Over the course of the years, seems I earned the nickname 'Dr. Food', so it would be fitting to have that title with my other list of credentials. Well, I decided, Let's just worry about getting my master's degree.

I was having some health issues right before my birthday and I thought it would be a good idea to treat myself to a holistic therapy: Chakra cleansing. Likely you are asking, *"A what? A Chakra cleansing?"* Let me explain.

Our body has energy centers (Chakras) along the spinal column, which are associated with various parts of the body. Chakras are spinning, wheel-like vortexes that draw energy into the body. It is believed there are seven main chakra centers each governing a physical, emotional, mental and spiritual health component as well as a color vibration. For example, the heart chakra governs the thymus gland. Its role is in controlling, and the functioning of, the heart, lungs, bronchia system, lymph glands and immune system as well as the arms and hands: It is associated with the color green.

Regardless, I thought a spiritual cleansing was a good idea since I was hitting a milestone birthday. I found a quaint little place, and I scheduled my appointment for a Friday afternoon. It seemed like a good way to end the week. Besides, Mark was hosting a poker party that night and I really didn't want to be there anyway. I also had plans to meet a gal friend for dinner and enjoy drinks afterward.

So, I arrive for my appointment. The treatment room was small with a fluffy throw rug, dangly beads were hanging from the ceiling and there were lots of spiritual knick-knacks. Of course, there was incense burning. I was instructed to lie on my back in the middle of the rug and she was going to hover her hands over each of my chakras and see where she felt imbalances or strong energy. As she got to my belly button area, she asked if I had stomach issues! Was my body so bad off I was emitting strong energy from my midsection? I told her yes, without giving her too much information, that I did in fact have belly issues and she moved on. She then proceeded to instruct me on how she wanted me to think, focus and how to visualize myself releasing negative energy. Honestly, it was uber hard for me to lay still, relax and focus. These things are not my strong qualities, so it really took some time to get into the session. But once I did, I totally enjoyed it!

Visual imagery is a powerful tool: It is something I used to do when I danced. I visualized myself completing the pirouettes or jumps. If one can see themself doing something, it can and will happen. I tried my best to visualize my stomach being released of the

Crohn's - I visualized myself with a healthy colon. I visualized myself releasing the color that corresponded with that area. This went on for a while. Then she changed gears and talked about bringing positive energy, white light and strength into my body. *Huh? How the hell do I do this?* Well, the same way one lets it go, they can bring it in. I visualized positive energy coming toward me and making me feel warm and happy. This, too, went on for a while, and then she left me to think about nothing. She asked me to clear my head and focus on silence, and nothing else. Really, where did she expect the 9,000 voices I hear to go? And where was the lists of to-do's suppose to go. And what if I have an itch? Can I move to scratch it? Overall, the session was relaxing, and I did feel better.

She left the room and left me to the silence that is never in my head. This was tough, so I tried to imagine myself floating on a magic carpet up in the sky and near the clouds. I was gently swaying in the breeze, light and airy, surrounded by pure white light from the sun. Guess it worked, I think I may have dozed off, but regardless it was a great experience.

Now, I was off to meet my friend for dinner and a drink. I was running a few minutes late so she went ahead and got us a table, and she had even ordered us a glass of wine. It was a sunny, warm May afternoon, so she chose a table out on the patio. I remember not wanting to order dinner right away, but my friend said she was really hungry and wanted to order before they got too busy. Ok, but what's the rush? I'm all relaxed and chillin', and she wants to be so speedy and fast. *Cool your jets sister.*

I ordered something anyway - salad I think - shocker, I know! What did you think I was going to order? A burger? Anyway, we chatted, and I told her all about my session and how relaxing it was, and how calm, warm and fuzzy I felt. Our dinner arrived along with another glass of wine. We enjoyed our meal and I wanted to order another after dinner *let's hang out* drink, but she was ready to go. Her phone rang and it was her hubby - he was at our house for poker - and they were out of, or needed something, and could we bring it to them? (Really, it is a bunch of guys playing poker - what could they possibly need?). We paid our bill and off we went. This was not turning out like I wanted: I was ready to stay out and play.

We decided it was best to go see what they needed, then go back out and get it. So, homeward bound we went. We pulled into the driveway, which was blocked with cars. We made our way toward the backdoor and upon entering I realized what was going on: Mark had thrown me a surprise 40th birthday party, to which I was officially 30 minutes late! The house was filled with family and friends. Wow, he wracked up some brownie points. Now, it all made sense - the rushing at the restaurant and that phone call was not from her hubby it was from Mark who was asking where in the hell we were. This was great, he threw a great party and totally had me surprised especially since my actual birthday was the following week.

The other big events in May were Tara's last day of school followed by an award's ceremony and her graduation party, which was here at the house. Eighteen years just flew by! In lieu of a graduation present we took a trip to the Big Apple. We hadn't been to New York and decided it would be fun, and it was. Everything from Times Square to Lady Liberty to Broadway to Central Park to Brooklyn was amazing. The streets never sleep and there was always something to do and see. The cars, taxis, busses and subways were always busy. The streets were constantly buzzing. It is truly a real melting pot. And if I might say, bras are totally optional there, as were manners.

We stayed around 65th Street near Central Park. We always liked to go to the museums and it was not really that far to get to 42nd Street. No matter where we went for vacations we always walked if we could and this trip was no different. We took in two musicals and at the time MOMA (Metropolitan Museum of Modern Art) was in Brooklyn, so we walked across the infamous Brooklyn Bridge. One day we walked all the way from Central Park down to Battery Park/Wall Street and back. Well almost: we got to the Broadway area, and Mark and Tara were about ready to kill me if we didn't stop walking and take the bus or subway. Well, if we hadn't been walking we wouldn't have had the chance to see John Mayer practicing in the park in preparation for his concert that night. We stopped to listen and when it was time to start moving, both Mark and Tara glared at me, "You aren't suggesting we continue walking?" OK, I stopped and we waited for a bus. Bus = Boring! But whatever! Overall, nine days in New York was MORE than enough!

Once back home it left us with less than two months before Tara took off for college, and I started my master's program. We took in a few baseball games, went to the Botanical Gardens and took the train to Chicago. We had a great summer. Tara's cousins came to visit: We swam and had a wonderful time. We shopped for her dorm room items and went out to eat all the time.

As for my day job/s, I was still involved in all the classes, trainings, home-health visits that I was before. I needed to figure out how to best manage my time. I decided to leave the PRN position at St. Elizabeth's Hospital. I rarely worked and when I did I didn't like it, so I gave my notice and turned in my badge and keys. OK: One less thing hanging over my head.

The biggest life issue right now was getting Tara off to college and settled. Remember, she is my pleaser and the gal who doesn't really like a lot of change. Well, guess what sister? This is going to be more change than you bargained for! She kept a stiff upper lip, but I knew she was worried. We even took a day trip to meet her new roommate so she knew with whom she would be rooming. As any parent knows, moving day is work! If it isn't the heat, it is the crowds and the confusion, and trying to get the room set up. And the worst: trying to get the computer compatible to the school's system. For the love, it couldn't be anymore challenging. August 19th, 2004 - I remember it well. Finally, after a long day we went out to grab a bite before we took off for the drive back home.

Leaving her there reminded me of her first day at pre-school: Her tiny little face, bangs and long hair, and hands were pressed against the glass - tears running down her face - you could almost hear her say, "Please don't go mommy, please don't go." I felt like I was leaving a part of me at EIU that day. After 18 years of togetherness, jokes, travels and fun, I felt lonely. Empty-nest syndrome is what they call it. Having only 20'ish years age-difference made me feel like we were sisters, not mother and daughter. There was 40 years difference between my mom and I: The two relationships were totally different.

A parent's job is to prepare their child for the real world. To be sure they have tough skin, but are still caring. You want them to have respect for others and respect their elders; to stand up for their beliefs and never ever let anyone tell them they are worthless or a bad person. Your child's behavior is a pure reflection of their upbringing: I hope I/we did our job well. I knew the next few days were going to be tough, but she needed to stick it out, as I knew she was going to love it once she got settled and into a routine.

Over the next few days there were many phone calls saying she made the wrong choice. She wanted to come home. She was not supposed to go away. She sent emails, too, which I printed off and have saved so one day I can read them to her. I did my best to comfort her and give her the confidence she could do it, and it would be OK. As for me, I was gearing up my first semester as a graduate assistant and student.

TWENTY-SEVEN

THE NON-TRADITIONAL STUDENT

Super-uber excited to get started on my master's. I had three classes I would be teaching: one walking class, and two strength training and flexibility classes. I had never created a syllabus before, so I structured mine based on what I had received when I was a student. Then I thought I had to come up with lesson plans and create the tests and quizzes. This really was going to be time consuming. Come to find out, there was always a GA who had been there a while and they were more than happy to give new GA's the low-down, and some of their materials. Fabulous! That surely would make it easier: I didn't have time to reinvent the wheel. I utilized the provided materials, modified them somewhat and changed all the dates. The more I read through the lessons and content order it was not really how I wanted to teach the class. I rearranged the format and information just a little. Now, I was ready. I was so eager to begin teaching these students what I knew, but what I found out was the students who signed up for these health and wellness classes thought they were blow-off classes. They assumed it was going to be an easy A. Clearly they have not met me; don't know me; and know that I don't and won't give an A unless it is earned. Amazingly I found I had to give points for attendance! These kids thought they were still in high school. They thought I was going to tell them when something was due or that a test was coming up. I didn't feel the material or the exams were hard. I expected the students to be on time, attentive and above everything else give nothing less than 100 percent effort. It is what I expected of myself and what I expected from them in return.

As for my own classes, I took three: Research Methods (explains how to write a thesis), advanced physiology and behavioral analysis, which included a lab. Right off the bat, I loaded up my plate. Plus, I had to offer office hours each week. As soon as I got my syllabus I would look over everything and decide which projects, or papers, I could start. I was eager to get started, but sometimes this comes back to bite one in the ass. I couldn't wait until the last minute either. Somehow I needed to figure out how to balance my time. The first month (September) was a bear and I found myself having a minor flare-up. Oh, what could have caused this? Stress? Too much work? Not enough rest? Or all of them? Anyway, it was short lived, and I carried on.

The beginning of October was EIU family weekend and, of course, we were going. She seemed to be settling in. She had four weeks under her belt; She knew her way around campus; and how homework she was up against. She and her roommate got along, but they weren't best buds. EIU had a fun-filled family weekend planned including a concert: Credence Clearwater Revival. Seemed an odd choice for a college, but I guess they were appealing to the parents rather than the students.

October quickly brought about midterms, which meant lots of studying! It also brought fall break, a surprise visit from our niece and the Cardinals were in the World Series. It also brought another minor flare-up. Guess I needed to think more about taking something else off my plate.

Since EIU and SIUE were state schools, Tara and I had our fall break week at the same time, which occurred during the week of Thanksgiving. We were able to shop, go out to eat and relax. Tara and I loved to watch the Macy's Thanksgiving Day. We would curl up under our blankets in our pj's to watch the bands and floats, and balloons as they marched down the parade path. Now, mind you, I couldn't sit still the entire two hours, so I would get up and do something during the commercials. Don't know why it is so hard for me to sit still; I really wish I possessed the ability to sit longer than a nanosecond and relax.

Thanksgiving Day at the Huntley household did not bring a big turkey dinner: It brought simplicity and togetherness. We aren't people who eat big meals and we aren't people who enjoy cooking, so why in the sam hell - on a holiday break - do I want to spend hours upon hours going grocery shopping, prepping, cooking and cleaning to eat a meal that isn't going to agree with me anyway? I don't, and I won't. If anyone wants to stuff a dead turkey carcass, go right ahead. I ain't stickin' my hand up any turkey's butt!

Before I knew it my first semester as a grad student was almost over. But the troubling part was I had to give exams, take exams and give presentations. How was this going to work? What I learned from this first semester was to have all the students turn in their work and take their tests BEFORE Thanksgiving break, that way I could focus on my tests and papers for the last few weeks. A lesson learned the hard way: Next semester will be different.

I decided to put up the Christmas tree early so I could enjoy all the lights and decorations. But truly this was a major pain in my ass. Tara was not home this year and Mark couldn't have cared less if we had a tree or not. I was on my own to decorate. I began the process of climbing into the attic to pull out the tree, then crawled into the other attic space to get the lights and the decorations. Mark liked the big lights; I liked the twinkle lights. I figured if I'm not getting any help, I'm putting twinkle lights on this tree! Then there are all the little sit-arounds and door decorations. Hours and hours later I was finally finished. The tree looked pretty, but I realized I had just lost many hours that could have been used studying!

I usually tried to have the family over for dinner for one of the holidays, and this year I picked Christmas. It was a tough year as it was the first Christmas without David. Mary Deane did put up their giant tree with decorations and all. We had our traditional Christmas Eve dinner at her house and the grandkids (who weren't so little anymore) still read the stories and hung the stockings. But this year we all hung out and drank a toast to good cheer. We let out all the little elf secrets and the games we used to play on them. They were adults now! Time to know the truth!

The New Year/Spring semester brought new courses to take and teach. Before I could get excited about them, I needed to get this eight-foot fake Christmas tree out of my living room! Note to self – DO NOT do this next year!

I received my grades and I was carrying a 4.0 (as was Tara!). I didn't want to ruin this, but the classes I was up against for the spring semester were horrendous. Not to mention the New Year always brings an influx of people who have resolutions to lose weight so attendance at the aerobic classes I taught grew substantially AND I was again offering my weight loss program at the YMCA as I did the year before.

I really was not concerned about the classes I had to teach as a GA (aerobics, step and Level I strength training). I knew how to set up the syllabus and I certainly knew how to teach an aerobics and step class. What I did have to worry about was taking an EKG class, a behavioral analysis II class and an exercise assessment class. Well two of three weren't bad, but I knew I didn't have any desire to go into clinical or cardiac rehab, so why in the hell do I need to learn how to read an EKG? This class frustrated the hell out of me. I learned best by sitting alone and working through the problems. I didn't do well sitting in a classroom being told I needed to figure out the problems before class was over. Now I'm not one to breakdown and lose my cool, but one day I lost it in class - I cried and walked out! I was so stressed over trying to figure out the EKG readings in class I couldn't even begin to verbalize to the professor my problem. He was cool when I talked to him the next day; he knew I knew my stuff and I would get it on my own time. A little embarrassing, yes. Did I care? No.

I'm not really sure how I survived that semester? I do know I welcomed spring break! At the end of March, Mark and I celebrated our 20th anniversary! Good golly, have 20 years gone by? I was now at the point in my life where I was married as long as I had been single. I have spent half my life with this man; guessing I picked the right one (or did he pick me?!).

During this semester I had to work on the study part of my thesis. I decided to pick a topic I could expand upon should I choose to get my Ph.D. I decided I wanted to know about the relationship between dose-related exercise and effects on self-esteem, and self-efficacy. Basically if one does more exercise do they feel better about themselves or worse? If I knew then what I know now, I would have opted for the comprehensive exit exam. Doing a thesis was a major pain in the ass and all my bound-final copy is doing is sitting on a shelf in the SIUE library collecting dust.

TWENTY-EIGHT

ONE YEAR DOWN AND ONE TO GO

Finals came and went and I earned A's in all of my classes. I had long given my students their finals and turned in their grades. The beginning of May brought some sense of accomplishment and freedom with the completion of my first year as a graduate student. A sigh of relief is all I felt and I was smiling ear to ear because I was still carrying a 4.0!

I thought this might be a good time to take something else off my plate and I decided to give my notice at BJC. I honestly never knew how far away the consults would be and the time it took to drive was time that was taken away from studying. While I enjoyed my position there, and I learned valuable information, the timing was no longer right.

My only real summer job was teaching aerobic classes at the YMCA, SIUE and a local health club. However, I was not totally free: I did teach an 8 a.m. walking class at SIUE and I took a thesis preparation class - but these were both fairly easy. I used the remainder of my free time to go to the pool with Tara. Oh, how I love swimming, floating and the sun!

Summer flew by. Before I knew it, it was time to pack up Tara's things and head back to EIU. She was totally enjoying college and felt comfortable, and confident. This is when the real empty-nest syndrome set in: She no longer needed me; she didn't call all the time; and actually days would go by before I would hear from her.

During the fall semester I was in full swing with completing my thesis, as I had to defend my outcome in front of my thesis committee before I could actually start collecting data. I had one more semester to go and I would be finished with my degree!!

I, once again, was given the aerobics class to teach; the walking class; and a new one - a physical health class. No problem. New challenges are always welcomed. August brought in new GA's and I was more than happy to share with them everything that was shared with me. My final few classes were a research class, an issues class, and of course the worst class possible: Statistics. That shit made no sense to me.

Not really sure why my advisor saved that class until the end? It seems it would have been more beneficial earlier on as I was planning my thesis and collecting data. But, what did I know?

Over the course of the last few years Mark had several jobs on his plate as well. He ran his own remodeling business and he eventually took over running a marina/bar on a private lake/community called Holiday Shores. This meant he was gone during the evenings and slept in late, while I was up and at 'em early and went to sleep early. Our paths crossed like two ships in the night. Our schedules couldn't be more different. But it worked for us.

Summers at the Marina were always super busy with people boating, floating, sitting on the deck (which Mark built), drinking and listening to the bands play their music. He enjoys what he does; he is good at what he does. As I said before there are a few things I think make for a happy and perfect marriage: Togetherness, independence and most importantly - separate bedrooms. There it's out. Mark and I have never, nor will we ever, sleep in the same room. Mark = TV on, volume up, stinky feet and he snores. Lorraine = TV off, silence, darkness, fresh air and no light. I need animation and stimulation during the day not when I'm sleeping.

Tara was settled into her sophomore semester and once again we went up for parent's weekend, went to the football game and out to eat.

My biggest hurdle now was the proposal for my thesis and the upcoming defense. This was the make-it-or-break-it scenario for my success, and ultimately, graduation. First, I had to get IRB approval and then finish the actual study; do the statistical analysis; and finish writing the thesis. All this pressure equaled stress, which equaled a flare up. I tried my best to be as compliant as possible. I took my plethora of medications. I had no problems swallowing many pills all at once. Otherwise, it would have taken forever! I tried to eat as cleanly as possible and I continued to carve out my own workout time. I not only needed it mentally, it really made me feel good physically. LIFE WITHOUT LIMITS! Let's see what this body is capable of if it is treated with kid gloves and lots of tender loving care. But seriously gut, this is clearly NOT the time to be flaring up on me.

I managed to get everything completed, turned in and my defense went well! I sum that up like it was a walk in the park, but anyone that has ever done a thesis knows damn good and well it is A LOT of flippin work! Now all that was left was walking across the stage and getting my diploma. I actually chose not to walk - did that with my bachelor's. I knew I was finished and I was now proud to say I had earned my master's degree. And no sooner than I received my diploma in the mail, I also received the warning signs that another flare up was impending!

The holidays that year were very low-key: no Christmas tree; no lights; no decorations; and no formal dinners to host. Finally, we had a year without holiday havoc and headaches.

To give myself a well-deserved break, Mark and I took a few vacations in Jan 2006 to get away from the cold and to see if it helped me relax. One can never go wrong going to Florida and California during the winter. The hardest part is coming home to the cold and potential ice and snow.

I was now officially free to do what I wanted to do, so I resumed teaching aerobic classes and I signed a contract to start working with our local firefighters. Now there is a group one would think would take pride in their health and fitness, but au contraire, not so much. My role was to help them attain a level of fitness that would ensure they pass their annual physical exams. There were just a few firefighters who were diligent with their workouts; a few that looked at me and said, "*Lady, I'm not going to change a thing*"; and then there were those who tried to make changes. Needless to say, I spun my wheels most days and unfortunately it was a futile effort.

Since I had my degrees, I was bound and determined to find a job I wanted to do and enjoyed. There was an open Assistant Manager position at the SIUE Fitness Center; it wasn't ideal, but I applied. If it was meant to be then I would get it, in the mean time I needed to figure out what I wanted to do. It was the first time in years I didn't have a carrot; I needed a goal! A mission! I needed a plan. I needed deadlines, timelines and projects. LIFE WITHOUT LIMITS.

TWENTY-NINE

MANY NEW VENTURES

The year 2007 brought nearly a gazillion new challenges and adventures. The biggest, scariest and ultimately most rewarding venture was opening my very own facility. Mark and I had been talking about it for months: How to make it financially and where would it be located. He made me go through the whole financial business process complete with a business plan, projections and a cost analysis. If I was serious I should have it written down and, besides, the bank would need that information anyway. He knows that if I come up with an idea, I will be off tackling it before the dust settles. I am on it. I'm ready to dig my feet in. No grass growing under my feet.

I looked into small business loans, government loans and sought private investors. After many meetings and much discussion, we decided to do it on our own. Even though the initial investment was scary, a place to call my own in the long run would all be worth it. With my own business, I wouldn't be spinning my wheels going to multiple facilities and being pulled in so many different directions. I would never know if it would work unless I tried. I knew I couldn't keep going 100 MPH every day. My Crohn's had flared so many times over the course of the last few years, likely due to the underlying stress of all my self-imposed commitments. I needed to consolidate and my thought was, If I build it they will come.

As they say in the marketing industry, "location, location, location." Mark and I looked at many places. Some were too small, some too expensive, some needed to be remodeled, some perfect but off the beaten path. Finally, we found a newly constructed building right on one of the main thoroughfares. It was perfect: a clean slate so I could create the perfect facility. Now the hard part was over and I had a location I knew exactly how much space I had to work with. I could start searching for equipment and as luck would have it, a friend was selling her home gym. She seemed to have much of what I thought I was looking for, though I really didn't know what I was looking for. The only items I wanted to buy new were the cardio equipment complete with warranty.

While we were working on getting the location ready in terms of painting, I was pondering the perfect name for my new business. A business name needs to imply what the business does and it needs to be catchy. And if selecting a name was not hard enough, there was the logo, too! Actually, it didn't take long before just the right name popped into my head: "Right Balance." Over the years I had found that I needed just the right balance between diet and exercise to stay healthy and keep my Crohn's semi-under control. A person can't eat like crap and then exercise like crazy: One can't exercise away a bad diet or poor food choices. There needs to be a balance. That part was easy. With my nickname being Dr. Food and the business name Right Balance, it almost implied the logo be a medical scales symbol. But I'm not really a doctor and I don't play one on TV, so the traditional scales were out, but what's to say I can't elaborate on that image? I'm not a graphic artist, so this designing a logo needed to be left to the professionals. I asked around and found a friend who had a friend who designed logos, so I passed along my ideas, my vision and mission and they created what I thought was a perfect first attempt.

All this business set-up seemed to be going too smoothly, though I was not complaining. The building build-out would be ready in no time. The rest was laying the flooring and moving in the equipment. While I waited on the building to be completed, I applied for the necessary permits and licenses, as well as getting my business name incorporated and my logo trademarked and registered. Good grief, this is exactly why I was so nervous about opening my own place; the cost and expenses were overwhelming. Every time I turned around I was spending money on something!

The day we chose to move the equipment, of course it snowed! Nothing like carrying heavy-ass weights in the snow, but that was the day we rented the truck and had the extra manpower so there was nothing we could do about it. Thanks Mother Nature, you are a real peach!

Finally, after a few short months of preparations, I was ready to open my doors. Such exciting times, I remember thinking: This is it! It is finally here. All I had been working for was coming to fruition. I could not have been more thrilled. I knew I wanted to send out a grand opening announcement. I set the date, created and mailed the announcement, crossed my fingers and hoped for the best.

As it turned out I had an amazing response! I was so happy; there were people I knew, people who had attended my aerobics classes, friends of friends and new folks I had never met. I was grinning ear to ear. I wanted to create something that was new and different, something that hadn't been done before. I created a private training facility where individuals could come to work out and feel comfortable knowing no one was watching them; they didn't have to wait for a machine, they didn't have to worry about other people's sweat, and they got my personal and full attention. I also differentiated my facility by making sure there were no contracts, no memberships and no monthly fees. People paid as they went.

Because of my education and credentials, if people needed nutritional guidance, I could help; if they were just diagnosed with diabetes, I could help; if they wanted to train for an event, I could help. I prided myself on making sure they got the individualized attention they wanted, needed and deserved. I never trained a client using the same workout over and over. Sure they will often see the same exercises, but they were always presented in a different way. If the body is one thing, it is ever changing and so should be the workouts!

I had no idea what to expect during the open house, but as good fortune would have it, I started scheduling trainings and assessment appointments. Before I knew it I had a very full schedule. I felt fortunate, blessed and grateful. I was doing what I was meant to do. People were calling on me for help; people were ready to make changes; people were responding to and following through with my recommendations. I couldn't have been happier.

As the first few months went by, I found I was training every bit of eight to 10 clients per day. There were those who liked to come in (6 a.m.) before work; those who came in after they dropped their kiddos off at school; and those that liked a noon-time workout. Early afternoon is usually when I would go home to regroup, make chart notes and plan my afternoon. I would grab a quick bite and then I was right back at it because as soon as school let out, the teachers came in; then those who got off work early; and finally those who came in right before and after dinner. I often trained until 7 p.m.-8 p.m. then went home to prepare for the next day and do it all over again.

I found some enjoyed when I worked out with them; they had just enough competitiveness in them that if I did "X" they wanted to do "XX." There were also those who didn't like to look at themselves in the mirror; those who wanted me to count for them; those who liked to count for themselves; and those who were disciplined enough that I created the workout and they executed said workout. Everyone was different in their approach and attitude toward fitness. Some liked to sweat — huffing, puffing and occasionally grunting. Some didn't like to sweat and some didn't sweat because their body didn't release heat as it should. That taught me to always be observant of anyone I was training and to always watch for signs that someone might not be feeling well.

Funny how less stress helps one feel better. I noticed my Crohn's was staying in check, but still giving me a few minor problems even though I was being compliant and taking my medications as directed. I was eating healthfully and, when time allowed, I was working out for myself. I decided to make a rather big personal change. I was going vegan! I had been vegetarian for years, but with the Crohn's issues I was having, I decided to take my eating habits to the next level (remember no gray, just black and white).

There are a few ways to approach being a vegan: some people go at it 100 percent and by that I mean they only wear natural fiber clothing (cotton, hemp); they wear natural rubber type shoes; and they don't wear any deodorants or makeup that contains animal products such as lanolin. They don't wear leather coats or have leather car seats. They don't use products tested on animals. Basically they are au-natural. Now I know I said no gray, but I really didn't see myself taking it to this extreme. I focused first on eliminating all animal ingredients from my diet. And, I would worry about the rest later.

How does one go about eating like a vegan? I never looked at this choice as to what I would be missing;

I looked at it as what I could have. All the fruits, vegetables, grains, legumes, nuts, soy and oils were options. It was rather complicated at first because if I selected a food product that had a nutrition facts label, I needed to know the various names manufactures used, i.e. maltodextrin, natural flavors etc., to describe their ingredients. Is the maltodextrin made from corn (or wheat)? And what about the natural flavors? Here is what I found as the definition of natural flavors taken verbatim from the Code of Federal Regulation, Section 101, Title 21, part 22:

> "The term natural flavor or natural flavoring means the essential oil, oleoresin, essence or extractive, protein hydrolysate, distillate, or any product of roasting, heating or enzymolysis, which contains the flavoring constituents derived from a spice, fruit or fruit juice, vegetable or vegetable juice, edible yeast, herb, bark, bud, root, leaf or similar plant material, meat, seafood, poultry, eggs, dairy products, or fermentation products thereof, whose significant function in food is flavoring rather than nutritional."

In other words, natural flavors can be pretty much anything approved for use in food. I figured if my body was having a difficult time digesting foods maybe it had something to do with all these natural flavors, i.e. processed crap. So I eliminated foods with a label that had natural flavors in the ingredient list.

Fruits and vegetables don't have labels. They are picked, shipped and available for consumption. Funny how these food items just sit in the produce section all colorful and bright waiting for you to sniff it, thump it, squeeze it, select it and take it home. They don't scream "I have fiber, I am trans-fat free, I am low-fat, I am fat-free" like most labels on all the processed food items do. Real food doesn't need to make a claim like boxed and/or prepackaged food items. A food should not have to advertise it is good, as food should naturally be good. Quote to ponder: "If it is made IN a plant, don't eat it; if it is made FROM a plant, eat it!"

The grains I included were usually rice, potatoes, yams, couscous, and other whole grains. These gave me the fiber I needed, and they made me feel full. Legumes were another story - I liked them but they often did not like me. Too much of the musical fruit and I was miserable. But, I was able to incorporate them into salads and as side dishes, just not as a main course. Nuts are so good and delicious, and I liked the crunch. Anything raw or natural was an option. I didn't want or need the nuts I ate to be coated in sugar or cocoa, or glazed. Really, who comes up with these ideas? Soy was yet another story. I soon found out a veggie burger isn't really any better than a processed burger. If one reads the ingredients on a veggie burger it might look something like this:

> Ingredients: Vegetables (mushrooms, water chestnuts, onions, carrots, green/red peppers, black olives), Textured vegetable protein (soy protein concentrate, wheat gluten, water for hydration), egg whites, cooked brown rice (water, brown rice), rolled oats, corn oil, calcium caseinate, soy sauce (water, soybeans, salt, wheat), contains two percent or less of onion powder, cornstarch, salt, hydrolyzed vegetable protein, corn, soy protein (corn, soy and wheat), autolyzed yeast extract, natural flavors from non-meat sources, sugar, soy protein isolate, spices, garlic powder, dextrose, jalapeno pepper powder, celery extract.

Now tell me how that is any better than a regular Angus beef burger?

Some other processed soy items such as soymilks were not any better either. Take this one for example:

> Ingredients: Organic soymilk (filtered water, organic soybeans), organic dehydrated cane juice, organic brown rice syrup and/or organic tapioca syrup, organic peanuts (roasted in organic peanut oil, salt), organic soybean oil and/or safflower oil, organic cocoa (processed with alkali), chicory root extract, vanilla extract, carbon bean gum, tapioca sugar, guar gum, carrageenan, natural flavors.

Maybe it was not the worst one out there, but there again is the term natural flavors. Thanks, but I'll pass on all processed soy items. If I want soy, I'll eat real soy foods such as tofu, tempeh, edamame, the real thing!

As for oils/fats, I included them on my salads as dressings or I used them in a stir-fry. Fat is a very important component in any diet, so I made sure I got my fair share, which include the necessary vitamins E and K, as well as essential omega fatty acids.

Something else people may not know about beverages is that wine is clarified with egg whites, so if I wanted to drink wine I needed to find a vegan wine. Or I could just drink a glass every so often. I was not really a fan of the hard stuff (vodka, whiskey, etc): Those burned my gut as they made their way through the alimentary canal. I can honestly say I have never had a beer in my life. I remember having a sip of my daddy's beer and I burped, felt bloated and didn't like the taste. Anheuser-Busch has never made a dime off of me! Now Mark on the other hand, well, he should have bought stock in the company.

While following a vegan diet, I never felt bored or deprived. Within a few weeks I began to notice less joint aches and arthritis. Related to taking out animal products? Possibly. Related to eliminating natural flavors? Maybe. Related to avoiding processed food?

Likely. Nevertheless, I felt better, and I was enjoying my newfound regimen.

Now one must remember, for most of my life food and I have always had a love-hate relationship. I looked to food purely as a necessity, not something that brought me pleasure. I ate because I needed to, not because I wanted to. I didn't care if it looked pretty on the plate or if it was even hot. I ate because I needed sustenance. Food to me was evil - I didn't enjoy it, and I didn't want to be miserable, so I ate only what agreed with me. And yes, sometimes this meant my diet was not necessarily balanced, but it was one I could tolerate and for me that was what mattered.

Looking back, going vegan was one of the best steps I took toward improving my health. I never did worry about finding vegan clothing or shoes, but I did eliminate all toiletries that contained any animal derivatives. I really don't worry so much about the wine, because most times I'm training and alcohol serves no purpose when a person is trying to gain strength or speed. This brings me to a carrot I went after in 2007 per the suggestion of a friend: Figure Competitions.

THIRTY

WHAT THE HECK WAS I THINKING?

I had never entertained the idea of figure competitions until a friend of mine suggested we give it a try. I really had no idea what I was getting myself into, but one shouldn't suggest something to me and not expect me to do it. I was not sure where to begin, but my friend had a coach, so I piggybacked off of her plan. However, there was one giant obstacle that was going to get in my way - the diet competitors followed consisted of a lot of protein, can you say chicken! Throw in some veggies, eggs, protein powders, the occasional piece of fruit and a half cup of oatmeal and there you have it. Well, we all know *that* diet was not going to happen.

I soon found out the lifestyle one must follow to be a figure competitor was nothing short of militant! The workouts were planned, the food was measured and calculated to the nearest ounce, and the number of supplements some competitors took was simply amazing! I took a lot of pills for my Crohn's already, I didn't feel the need to take anymore. Plus most of the supplements had capsule coatings that were made from animal gelatin (a byproduct of collagen and other connective tissues of the animal) GROSS! I'll pass, thanks! I'll just eat what I can and exercise my ass off.

Which brings me to the workout portion: it required cardio in the AM and the PM. Seriously! Who has time for that? I am running my own business - I have a hard enough time getting in one cardio session let alone two. As for the lifting, the workouts were designed to target one body part a week, and one could focus on the parts they think needed more attention or muscular growth.

I set my friend and myself up on a 14-week regimen and created the diet. We were ready to start this journey. Little did I realize there were other costly items that needed to be purchased. First there is the competition suit - basically a bikini embellished with rhinestones - kind of like my showgirl costumes. Then, there were the five inch stilettos, complete with clear plastic straps and clear heels, which made me feel like

I should be dancing around a pole! The other expenses were travel, spray tanning, entrance/membership fees and jewelry. About $800 later, I was ready, and this was without supplements and all that chicken!

I think the best part about training for a show, and the part I was looking forward to the most, was the fact I was going to be back on stage! That is the part most gals were afraid of especially in their teeny-weeny bedazzled bikini. That part was a breeze for me, but I did need to learn how to pose as there were very specific poses each organization required.

We began our 14-week adventure and hoped for the best. The Caveman Classic competition was in July in Arnold, Mo. (close to home). No real travel expenses were involved, so that was nice. I buckled down and got into my new cardio and lifting routine. I followed a strict diet (like being a vegan wasn't what some would consider strict anyway), and I drank the appropriate amount of water. I found a used competition suit online, and I ordered my shoes. All that was left was to practice my posing and get spray tanned.

Funny thing about these shows is one ends up seeing the same competitors over and over again, but the hardest part about competing was figuring which category to compete in. Options were *open*, *master's*, and *novice*. Since it was my first show I was able to enter the novice category and I also entered the master's division.

Since I was so new to this *sport*, I read blogs and looked at videos and pictures of prior contests. However, nothing prepared me for show day. What I learned was: one can never be tan enough; one can never practice their posing enough; one can never be sure how their body will respond; one will never know who they are up against; and one will never know exactly what the judges are looking for.

I also learned the tanning products rubbed off on everything; one shouldn't use bikini bite (glue that holds the suit in place) until after one has gone to the bathroom; that it feels like an eternity between the pre-judging show and the evening show; and that after a show a drink of alcohol goes right to one's head.

Fast forward 14 weeks and show-day had finally arrived. We drove to the venue, picked up the swag bag and got our number. Then we waited for the show's promoter to hold a meeting telling us the order of the competitors and what time to be back for the evening show. After that we were allowed to go backstage and get ready. Well, it was only 8:15 a.m. - pre-judging didn't start until 10 a.m. and I was in the eighth group to go onstage. That means it could be noon before anything happened. *What in the hell am I supposed to do for four hours?* Well, you wait and make small talk with the other competitors. Some are nice, some are shy, some are bitchy and some are there to WIN. Everyone is in his or her zone. Whatever, this was a carrot for me, nothing I ever wanted to do again, and it was something I could check off my bucket list (even though I didn't know it was on my list) and move on to something new. I was there to have fun, not win.

There were three gals in my division. Girl #1 clearly had done this before and was in it to win it. Girl #2 was softer than me, thinking it was her first or second show, and then there was me. I was not big, I didn't have boobs (actually what I had had melted away a few months ago); I didn't have the definition that I think the judges were looking for. What I did have was stage presence and a great smile. When it was my turn to go out there, I strutted my stuff. I smiled like I owned the joint, and I stood proud and tall. I worked hard for what I had and I wanted to show it off. As it turns out, I came in second and brought home two giant trophies (which are still collecting dust in the basement). I was so happy when the show was over, I wanted some alcohol. I hadn't had a drink in over 14 weeks and mama was thirsty. Needless to say the excitement of the day and the dehydration from contest prep made my glass of vino go right to my head. That didn't stop me from having two, especially since my gal friend who had come to see the show was also my chauffeur for the evening.

I swore I was selling the suit so I wouldn't be tempted to compete again. Well, the suit, shoes, tanning products and other assorted gear was shoved into the back of my closet. I shut the closet door and thought - *Well, now that is over what shall I do next?*

So many of my clients had seen me go through this show preparation process; they were a little intrigued and asked questions. Somewhere in the back of my mind I was already thinking, *Maybe, just maybe, I'll do this again.* But until that time came, I needed to find another carrot.

As good fortune would have it, I was so busy at the studio I didn't have time for much else. I worked very hard to build a reputable business. I didn't want anyone else working for me. I wanted things done my way, because it was ultimately my name that was going on everything. I took great pride in what I did and how I ran my business.

Remember when I worked at the hospital how frustrated I was because I had to work the traditional 9-5 when I was so able to do the work in five hours. Remember how it took an act of congress to create programs and handouts? Well, now I could do all this on my own time and at my own speed. Working alone appealed to me even though it meant I was the accountant, marketing manager, scheduler, trainer, advertising agent, legal consultant, etc. I wore all the hats, but that was OK because then I knew that everything was just like I wanted it.

I found myself picking up some additional contracts with larger businesses and corporations. I would offer a smorgasbord of services they could choose from and incorporate into their wellness programs. I offered Lunch 'n Learn classes as well as monthly classes, supermarket tours and, on occasion, in-home consultations. I worked with some local physicians who would refer their patients to me if they thought they would benefit from my services. I was also responsible for putting together a collaborative effort between a large St. Louis-based orthopedic group and local trainers so the physicians could refer their patients to the trainers in hopes of diminishing the possibility of surgery. I always had many projects going at one time. I welcomed the opportunity, challenge and potential for reaching more people. LIFE WITHOUT LIMITS: One won't know unless they try.

Even though I had an office to go to, I still worked quite a bit from home. I revised programs, created newsletters, followed up on trainings and new client referrals – you name it, I still did it. There is a lot one can accomplish between the hours of 4:30 a.m.-6:30 a.m. (which is when I usually left for the studio).

As the months/years unfolded and I got into a routine at the studio, I was better able to start looking for that next carrot. Seems as though two years just flew by - how does the saying go? Time flies when you're having fun! Well, that I was. My Crohn's was in check. One can deduce that maybe - just maybe - the transition to the vegan diet had something to do with it. My daily medications remained the same and so far my doctors were pleased with my status quo status.

But, I was in need of some structure; I felt I was floundering with my own workouts...no direction...no goal and certainly no carrot. Oh, what do I do? Lo and behold there was not a shortage of ideas once I started looking and asking around. I decided I would start running again. I use that word loosely; I don't run, I jog. I would run if a bear was chasing me or from a burning building, but otherwise, let's just say I jogged. Our town, small as it was, had no shortages on races. In the spring of 2010 I found the perfect event on my birthday weekend. What a better way to celebrate than to get out and be active. I printed off the registration form, recruited a group of gals/clients to run the race with me. We had team shirts made - we called ourselves the "Right Balance Racers." We entered the 5K (3.1 miles) and we had a blast. That prompted me to participate in a variety of other local races over the course of the next few months. There were a few 5K's, which turned into 10K's (6.2 miles), which turned into a half-marathon (13.1 miles). I went from not running at all to running like a mad woman (again, no gray, just black or white).

Like I said earlier, when I picked a carrot, usually, others ask about it. Well, I had one particular client who worked as hard as I did and she decided she wanted to join me in running the half-marathon. I had many friends who were seasoned runners and who had competed in many races and for many causes, but this was all new and uncharted territory for me. So my friend/client and I picked an event together. I had heard a lot about the Rock 'n Roll (RNR) running events. They were held throughout the year and all over the U.S. The premise of the event was there were bands that played at each mile (hence the name Rock 'n Roll), and there was usually a celebrity to MC the event. We picked an event not too far from home and during the summer. I liked the heat, and really, no matter if you run in the winter or summer, it was always going to be at the mercy of Mother Nature. We picked the RNR Chicago half-marathon: We printed, completed and mailed in our registration form.

I always found that completing and sending in the registration form was the only way one was truly committed to participating in any event. Otherwise, one could always come up with some excuse not to do the workout, but not me. The form was mailed and August first would be my first half-marathon. The training went well, the problem I had was with shoes.

From all my years of ballet and pointe shoes, I didn't want any running shoe that was snug to my foot. I wanted wiggle room. My very first pair of shoes (as it turns out) was the shoe I would ultimately fall in love with. But, as I racked up the miles, I decided (don't ask me why) I needed to try a different brand of shoe. Once again going into this adventure blindly, I changed shoes two weeks before the race. And as any runner reading this knows, rookie mistake!

My role as dietitian, trainer, motivator and cheerleader was to inspire others, I often didn't really think I was reaching others or impacting them with what I was personally training for. But when my family, friends and clients saw me struggling with the many up's and down's I had with Crohn's, and I kept going, allowing myself NO EXCUSES and following through with my motto LIFE WITHOUT LIMITS, I was imparting the inspiration they needed to get moving. I never really put two and two together until recently that what I do and the voracity with which I do it, helps others find the strength and energy they need to get moving. I never really looked at myself in that way; I just did what I had planned: Remember - NO EXCUS-

ES. I just did it. Another event was not any different than the last event or the next event.

All my years of rehearsals, classes and performances, instilled in me the discipline needed to finish the job I started - no matter what obstacles got in my way.

Back to the running shoes and my first big race. My friend and I decided to take the train. Our hotel was booked and our running gear ready. We took the early train so we made it into downtown Chicago by noon and to the Expo before it closed so we could pick up our swag bag of goodies. Who doesn't like tons of free items? Since we just spent five hours on the train, we decided we would walk the three miles from our hotel to the convention center. We needed to move our legs. But, it was not our legs that bothered us, it was the fact we wore flip-flops! Needless to say we took the shuttle back to the hotel as blisters were not what we needed right now.

No matter what event or show one has planned, one never really gets a good night's sleep. Nerves and adrenaline are in high gear. For me it was not so much the nerves, I was concerned as to what my belly was going to do. At home I had a great morning routine but when one is traveling, everything is different. The fact we had to be at the race early made me hope and pray my belly was not going to give me fits! Of course the first thing I scope out are the location of the bathrooms or in this case the port-a-potty's.

Wow, this is a site to behold. There were thousands upon thousands of runners lining the streets of Chicago. Our guest MC was none other than Mr. Al Roker. Of course there were so many people that I never actually got to see him, but I heard him. We all made our way to our respective corral spots, I wished my friend good luck and then tied, and retied, my laces for like the ba-zillionth time. They had to be just right! Not too tight, not too loose. Oh, and did I have to go to the bathroom one more time?

Finally, it is my turn for our corral to take off. I had been to Chicago a few times before, but never along this particular route and certainly not at this speed. We ran about five miles through downtown before turning up Michigan Avenue and heading toward the Shedd Aquarium. There we made a loop to head back toward downtown.

I am at about mile eight and I hear my name.... *"Hey, Lorraine."* I'm thinking – really, there is another Lorraine right here in the race next to me? Out of all these people is there really another Lorraine? So I look around and don't see anyone, but then in the crowd lining the sidewalk I see a friend frantically waving at me. Wow, that was too funny. Never expected to hear my name and certainly didn't expect to see a familiar face in the crowd! I waved and smiled, and gave him two thumbs up and off I went.

As we began to make our way back downtown, I observed all the people running the race. There were old, young, slim and not-so-slim runners. There were people who passed me, then would walk and I'd pass them, and we would repeat this pattern. There were people pushing strollers who passed me, and a man with a prosthetic leg who also passed me! *Good grief, really?? Yay for you, but I must suck at this?* What I learned was that runners come in all sizes and shapes. Never judge and never assume a runner is faster or slower than you or that you can beat them.

My goal for my very first event was to finish! I really was not too concerned with my time, and I'm glad I was not because my new shoes were coming back to bite me in the butt. At about mile 10 my feet, then my shins and calves, started going numb. Crap. I tried to keep going, but I couldn't feel my feet. I walked a little and tried to shake them out, and did this for the next mile or two. Finally, I said, *"Screw it, I'm just going to run and hope for the best."* As we all rounded the corners, the crowd was shouting "almost there," "keep going," "you can do it." The cheering from the crowd was my favorite part. So many spectators with signs and whistles and cowbells; it was truly amazing. And then finally, I saw the finish line with the giant banner spanning across the street, and I started to get emotional. I picked up some speed and sprinted toward the finish line, and as I crossed the line, I broke into tears. No, I was not broken; no, I was not hurt; and no, I was not sad. I'm not really sure why I cried, but I did. Sense of accomplishment? Sense of completion? Sure, maybe. But I did it: I got my medal and smiled for the cameras. I rose to the challenge and finished. It was not about winning; I knew I was not going to do that! What mattered more is what I did to prepare. The journey, the process, the determination and the dedication, that is what defines a person!

Now that I have crossed the finish line, the hard part was trying to find my friend in this vast sea of people! We finally saw each other, gave each other a big giant sweaty hug and sat down! After we cooled down and calmed down, we hobbled back to the hotel, rested for a bit, showered, packed, checked out and made our way to get something to eat. Didn't really care where we ate, the closest place at this point was the best! The less I had to walk the better. We had a few hours to kill before we made our way to the train station for the five-hour ride back home. Note to self: NEVER EVER take a train and sit for five hours after you run 13 miles. Talk about getting stiff!

The ride back gave us a chance to ponder our next carrot. I was leaning toward a full marathon. My friend was not sure. As soon as I got home, I found the next do-able race and started planning my training schedule. I was pumped and psyched to have a new carrot. A new journey! A new challenge!

What I didn't give myself was a break. I went right into increasing my running miles the next week. I went back to my old favorite running shoes and cursed the ones that made my feet go numb. Well, it wasn't but a few weeks into my new training regimen when something happened that really put a damper on my progress.

THIRTY-ONE

OH, WHEN WILL I EVER LEARN?

The year 2010 brought me many rewarding and fun-filled experiences. It was late August and a friend and I were enjoying a day of floating and boating, and drinking at the lake. The weather was perfect, the water was just right and the sun was shining. What more could you ask for on a Sunday afternoon? As we were floating - getting knocked around by some occasional waves - my friend decided it would be a good idea to swim to the Marina. OK, I said, but there should have been many red flags going up here: (A) my friend doesn't really swim; (B) she has been drinking; and (C) the Marina is at least three-fourths of a mile away. Well, I won't go into details, but after the first 10 minutes guess who was dragging who? My friend is giggling and all happy jack, and I was yelling at her to move her arms, kick her feet and swim, dammit, and not worry about getting lake water in her drink. So this great idea (yes, that I agreed to) became a three-hour tour (well, not really just sounded fun to say) from hell.

Mark, who usually bartends on Sundays, saw two people on rafts coming into the No-wake cove. He watched for a few moments and then said to the people at the bar, "How much you want to bet one of those people is my wife?" And sure enough, there we were, laughing and happy, one of us drunk (not me) and one of us sober (me). I pulled, drug and hauled my friend's happy ass over three-fourths of a mile!

On our journey that day something didn't feel right with my hips. I'm not really sure what didn't feel right, but something hurt. Was I kicking too hard? Was it because I was swimming sideways at times? Not sure. I chalked it up to doing all the work and carried on with my day.

Monday was a rest day from running, which gave my body a chance to recover. The following day I was ready to go for my run. I got dressed, tied and retied my shoe laces, and headed out the door only to be stopped dead in my tracks when I took my first few steps. I couldn't put any weight on my right leg. What was wrong? Why did it hurt so? Noooooooo!

If you remember I mentioned earlier I had collaborated with an orthopedic group in St. Louis, so I called and told them what was going on. Why didn't I just call my doctor one might ask? Well, something in the pit of my stomach told me what was wrong, so instead of beating around the bush, I went right to the source. They suggested I get some X-rays and an MRI. I did what I was told. Then I brought the films and CD images with me to their office, only to be told what I thought and really didn't want to hear. Yup, I had a stress fracture! *Are you sure? Are you certain? Really? Look again please. I have to train for a marathon.*

Long story short, the doctor that saw me knew of me, as his best friend's wife attended my boot-camp classes. He knew how hard I worked out and what I expected of those who came to my class. He tried in no uncertain terms to tell me I needed to stay off my leg, period. End of conversation. But before he could get another word in, I interrupted him and said to him, "Doc, I am likely not going to follow your orders, so if you want me to be off my leg for four months, you need to tell me eight, if I need to be off my leg for two months, then tell me four. He got the picture. He proceeded to tell me stories of what happened to other (obsessive compulsive) runners who didn't follow orders. He also told me I had a few strikes against me since I am a smaller-framed vegan with Crohn's who in my mid-40's taking on ventures for which my body was not ready. Yeah, yeah, yeah, Doc - I got it! OK, so I need to be off my leg for four months. Crap, that will take me into the winter; What if it snows? What if it is icy? How will I manage to get around with crutches? I have NEVER used crutches before! This ought to be interesting since I like doing things at warp speed; this certainly is going to cramp my style!

Clearly, I was not prepared for life on crutches! And thank goodness I had a couple of interns who were helping me at the studio. Yes, I didn't mention that before, but each semester I tried to be a mentor for a student going through the kinesiology program at SIUE. I had two great gals working at the studio, they helped out with a variety of things, such as doing research, putting together pseudo workouts for clients and then I would explain why the workouts would or wouldn't work. They observed me training and teaching; they were really godsends to say the least.

First order of business was getting a pair of crutches. I was still allowed to drive even though the injury was to my right leg. I quickly learned the best ways to get in and out of cars, buildings and the back door to my house. It was amazing to me how many places didn't have automatic doors or the door springs were wound so tightly the door slammed into me as I was trying to get in or get out of the building. Then, there was the small task of carrying things. I had my big work bag that held all my schedules and medicines; my phone, my keys and my water bottle. Hmm, last time I checked I didn't know how to juggle, but my hubby - the quick thinker the he is - found me an 'S' hook. This attached to the crutch handle and had a hook at the other end for me to hang my belongings. However, too much stuff equaled a lopsided, unbalanced gait, so the hook served as my key, and water bottle holder. I emptied my workbag and started using a backpack, and I started wearing clothes with pockets. Little changes that made life much easier. I am certainly not going to let a little thing like crutches slow me down. If there's a will, there's a way!

Now, there was the small matter of running my studio. Most, if not all, the people who trained with me had been with me for awhile. They knew how things worked, how I worked and how I wanted them to work, so it was not too difficult going about my daily business and training routine. The real difference was they had to get the weights or equipment out, and they had to put it away: consider it part of the warm-up and cool-down! Everyone was super helpful and understanding. They knew there was no one more frustrated than me at this whole situation. A few weeks went by and I was doing fine, getting used to the fact that I had to remember everything I needed upstairs because once I got downstairs, I was not going back up. Life went on as usual.

The part I missed the most was doing some sort of cardio! It was easy to continue lifting and strength training: I could do that sitting down. But I needed some cardio, and sure enough the perfect thing came along. I had recently ordered some heavy ropes and they arrived just in time to save my sanity. I could use these 30 or 50 feet ropes sitting down, and slamming them to the floor made for an awesome cardio (and arm) workout. I didn't trust myself using the ropes while seated in a chair, so I sat on the floor, but getting up and down was no easy task. I ultimately settled for the chair and modified the moves. The ropes got a lot of use for a while by me and everyone else.

Another thing I remember that was not easy was showering, but with a little engineering and a chair, that, too, became no problem. Thank God it was a mild fall and winter. There really was not any snow and it barely rained. I couldn't even imagine if I had had to try and maneuver crutches, bags and all my other gear through raindrops or snowflakes.

December was quickly approaching, which meant I was due back for some follow up X-rays and another MRI. From the looks of the images and the fact I followed orders (believe it or not!), I was released from the crutches and able to move around freely. I really wanted to do the dance of joy. The doc still discouraged any jogging at this point. I was chomping at the bit to get back to running, but then a friend made a comment that stuck with me. She said, "You have not run in how many years, so what's a few more weeks or months?" Wow, she knew me and knew exactly what to say: Her words made perfect sense. I put aside the running until the spring; besides it was cold outside and this lady doesn't run in the cold.

THIRTY-TWO

TRAVELS, NEW CARROTS AND...

With the Marina closed for the winter, Mark and I had time to take a few trips to sunny, warm destinations. And this year was no different; in fact we took two trips. It was nice to have the ability to close the studio, but what was not nice was that when one doesn't work, one doesn't make money. I had issues with letting go, but this year - with two interns - I decided to give it a try and let them at least teach classes while I was gone. And imagine this, it all worked out. The world didn't end, the classes went well and everyone was happy. Baby steps!

It seemed the studio never really had a lull or an influx of people wanting to train. Seems there was always something or some occasion (wedding, vacation, reunion) that people wanted, or needed, to get in shape for. My schedule was always consistent and for this I was grateful.

With the holidays behind us, our trips over and my hip healed, I was ready for another carrot. I knew that running needed to wait until summer, so what else could I do? *Hmm. Let me see. I don't know, what about another figure competition?* The same gal I ran in Chicago with was searching for a new goal as well. However, she was scared as hell about doing a show. For her it was not about the training, cardio or diet, it was getting up on stage in the suit and heels. But she wanted to do something outside of her comfort zone and a show was it. So we picked a show, filled out the registration forms, sent in our money and committed to competing. I was not about to let her get onstage alone; I was going to be sure I was there with her every step of the way. Didn't I say I was not going to do this again? Well, I never sold my suit, so always lurking there in the back of the closet was temptation.

The show we picked was in Kentucky in mid-February. This show was also one of the biggest shows around and had upward of 350 competitors, which was three times the size of the Caveman show I did in Missouri. Based on my previous workouts and experience with training, I knew I needed to change my lifting routine so I could gain more muscle mass! I was still following my vegan diet and doing my cardio. I stuck with it for weeks, did my best and gave it 200 percent, but I really didn't feel like I was getting anywhere. I was not getting bigger, so I did try a few supplements to see if it helped. Really, all it did was give me gas and make my belly hurt. But, it is only for a few weeks, so let's see what happens.

Show weekend arrives and we gather our gear and hit the road. I have never been one for directions nor have I ever been good at reading a map. My philosophy was to aim my car in the right direction and eventually I would get there. This was a far cry from what my friend thought. We crossed into Kentucky and she asked if I knew what exit I was taking. I said, *"Yes, the one with the brown sign that says convention center."* She eyeballs me and says, "And the exit number is?" Well, hell I don't know but I'm pretty sure there is only one convention center in town: Can't be that hard to miss. I saw the exit sign, and she asked – "You know how to get to the hotel right?" I respond by saying, "No, but it is directly across from the convention center." Clearly not the answer she was looking for. But as luck would have it, it was a small town and we drove right to it! "See, no worries!"

The weekend was fantastic; there were 12 women in the master's (meaning over 40) division, in which I chose to compete. Really, 12 women who were ripped and looked better than most 20-year-olds. Why couldn't I have picked the Open division? There were fewer girls in that division. Again, one just never knows! I didn't place, but my friend did. She was ecstatic and I was thrilled for her. She overcame a huge fear and succeeded.

Competing in this show made me realize I liked the structure of training; I liked being on stage; I liked (and disliked) the fact one never really knew who they were going to be competing against; and that made me work harder. What I didn't like was the fact I didn't feel like I belonged in the Figure division. The more I trained and lifted, the leaner I got and that really was not what the judges were looking for. A figure competitor should have overall muscle tone with shapely lines, overall firmness, but not be excessively lean. Basically some definition without looking cut.

However, my physique and vegan diet made me too lean, plus most of the girls in the figure division had some serious *girls* if you know what I mean. I had two layers of foam in my top with lots of bikini bite to hold my *girls* in place. So what to do? The only other division to try at the time was the bodybuilding. Actually, the show promoter suggested I might do well in that division. They compare your body against you, not against the gal next to you. *OK if you say so, I'll try that class next time.* The bodybuilding categories were divided into two (sometimes three) weight classes, under 125 pounds and over 125 pounds. So maybe, I had a better fighting chance.

On our five-hour drive home, we had much to discuss; doing another show, training for another half marathon. Somehow the hours flew by. We were still dehydrated from the previous day's show preparation, so we didn't need to make any pit stops. I decided I was going to give bodybuilding a try. The closest and earliest show was in May - in Kansas City. If I was going to be humiliated, I didn't want to do it in town.

I began and did my homework on how to pose for bodybuilding (which is quite different than figure posing) and took mental notes of the competitors' photos from previous shows. Honestly, some of the bodybuilding gals were kind of scary. I'm thinking these gals ate a lot of chicken! Once again, I was not going to change from my vegan diet! My belly wasn't really giving me any fits, and if it was I was so accustomed to it I didn't notice. I found a great vegan protein powder made from hemp, chia, rice and pea protein. I used nutritional yeast on my rice and potatoes, and I belonged to a food co-op, so I had plenty of fresh veggies and herbs. I used my nut butters and rice, or crackers as snacks. The thing I have always missed most was cheese! An Italian without cheese is like a fish out of water. Most vegan cheese is waxy or didn't melt. I finally found a brand I could live with, but it really was not the same.

In the bodybuilding division, participants don't wear high-heeled shoes, they go barefoot. The suit is plain and the jewelry is minimal. No biggie. One still needed to have stage presence and that was not a problem. I changed my lifting routine again and I did my cardio as suggested. I really didn't tell a lot of people I was doing this because, honestly, I was nervous about being on stage next to Helga.

Surprisingly I placed third in the May show and won a giant sword! Better than a trophy or medal, at least the sword made for a good topic of conversation. Placing third gave me the courage to try the division again. I wanted to tweak my lifting routine. Let's see what happens if I lifted as heavy as I could. The constant was still the diet.

I found another show right here in St. Louis and began a new training program. I had two months to see what kind of progress I could make. But the very best part was I had another gal join me. She, too, was self-motivated; she traveled but was still able to get in the required amount of training. It was so much fun to have another person there. I remember show day like it was yesterday. The venue was in a downtown hotel that had a theater. There were lots of participants and we met, and made, some new friends. We were pumped. Neither of us placed at that show. And surprisingly, there were seven women bodybuilders in the division! Seems just as I find a division I think would fit me, everyone else joins in on the party. I looked at the show as yet another experience and learned more and more from the other competitors.

Now that I had done three shows I was bitten by this competition bug. I wanted to try again and October brought another local show. This time there were five other gals who wanted to give this competition thing a try. I created their workout regimens based on their strengths and weaknesses. We had weekly practice posing sessions; they followed a strict meal plan; and they stayed focus and driven the entire time. I was so proud of those girls. They dug in deep and gave it all they had. When show time arrived we all carpooled to St. Louis. We were tan; we had our arsenal of show gear; our food; and our abundant energy.

As it turned out this was a rather large show, too! But the gals did great, some placed and others did not. I actually came in second in the Open division. The closest I had been. I felt the show was judged fairly as others in the same division were much more muscular than I. This gave me the urge to keep on trying. I did try one more time at the end of October. Two of the gals decided to give it another whirl, too, and joined me in a late October show. It is amazing how the different organizers of these shows can make or break a show. Some shows you leave saying, "Wow, I will definitely do that show again." And other shows you want to ask the promoter if it was their very first (rodeo) attempt at running a show.

In this show there were only two of us in the bodybuilding division. There were nine judges. I didn't win, but did find out four of the judges placed me first and four placed my competitor first. So even though I didn't win, I felt I was very, very close, and that made me feel that all my hard work paid off. After that show I decided to call it quits, plus there aren't many shows during the winter months, so we all decided to give our bodies some well-deserved rest. But, I don't rest well. I was already thinking about what would come next.

There was talk in the competition world a new women's division was going to be introduced called "Women's Physique." They said they were looking for women who didn't look like a bodybuilder, but had more muscle than a figure competitor. Well, this could be my division! I determined I would try one more, and hopefully, final show. I wanted to give this new division a try. I did in March and there were just a few women in this new division, we all looked extremely different and I do not feel we were judged fairly. That is when I decided to call it quits on the whole bodybuilding/competition thing. I was tired of judges judging me. I knew how hard I worked; I knew how clean my eating was; I knew I gave the training 200 percent. Don't sit there and judge me, and tell me I was not lean enough or big enough or... "Phooey on you, Mr. Judge." I won, I did it, I earned the right to call myself a winner. With this show, I ended my bodybuilding career. I gave two solid years of lifting heavy things and putting them back down. I did not drink and I did not eat anything I was not supposed to. I did everything to the letter.

For now I'll keep my suits, heels and other assorted show products tucked in the back of the closet. Maybe when I turn 50 and can enter into an older division I'll try again, but until then, this gal is done.

Spring and summer of 2011 were rather routine. I had been doing lots of walking and as any other summer brings; swimming and laying out! Oh, how I love summer. One day I decided I would walk to Holiday Shores. I was curious how long it would take. The weather was great so off I went. I knew it was about 10 miles as it usually takes about 15 minutes to drive there. I discovered it took two hours and eight minutes to walk there. Well, now I can check that off my list of things I have wanted to try.

My work schedule remained about the same. I gave a few nutritional talks, participated in some health fairs and worked on some projects. Of course my favorite season always seems to go by the fastest, and before one knows it, the leaves are changing and the mornings are darker. I am such a creature of the sun; I would love to live in a glass house!

In September I did something I had always wanted to do. A friend asked if I wanted to join her and go to a psychic party. Some friends of hers hired this lady and she was going to give readings. I thought, "What the heck, I'll go and see what she has to say." When we arrived, there were quite a few people waiting. Some readings took five minutes; some took 15 minutes. It was finally my turn. I walked into this small room to see a lady with long stringy gray hair sitting at a card table. She was wearing old and very tattered clothes, and she was not wearing any shoes. I'm thinking to myself, *You have got to me kidding me!* I introduced myself and she asked what I wanted to know. I thought, You are the psychic, tell me what you see. She was unable to offer spontaneous information, and only able to tell me things after I asked her a question. *Hell, lady I can do that!* She told me my car tires needed air - I had a bad knee - a female was always with me - that I was going to sign a contract but I needed to revise it first - I was going to go on a journey - that I had a peeping Tom (but he was gone) - and I needed to finish writing my book. Wow, random thoughts! This reading took all of seven minutes. Good thing it was only $20 bucks. Recap; my car tires were fine - my knees didn't hurt - I had not signed any contracts - had not taken any journeys - and had not seen any peeping Tom's. The only thing I had done is finish a book - a cookbook that is.

That session got me thinking, "I would like to try that again, but this time with someone more - reputable." I asked friends and searched the web and decided to schedule an appointment with a lady who lived in St. Louis. She offered a variety of reading and energy work. In December I called and scheduled a session. Let's see what she has to say: Hoping to get more info than flat tires and peeping Tom's! I was not nervous or scared. I was not afraid she would conjure up evil spirits or send negative vibes. I went with no expectations and no preconceived ideas. As soon as I entered this woman's house I was welcomed by the presence of *something*. I felt as though I had two energies wandering around with me. Not threatening in any way, they were just there. A friend went with me and the psychic did her reading first. But, the entire time, I felt these two energies. Now it was my turn. Again, not sure how or what she was going to do. But as soon as I walked in she asked me, who the little boy was that followed me in. I said I had no idea, but I wanted to know who the other two were that were following me around her waiting room. She paused and said one was my Indian spirit guide, and the other was my celestial female guide. She explained my spirit guide was with me all the time – he watched over me and kept me safe. The other celestial energy was from Pleiades, a group of stars referred to in Greek mythology as the Seven Sisters. The Pleiades have been around for hundreds of years. Maybe that explained why I was (or acted like) an old soul. Hmm, heard that before. Maybe being an old soul was a good thing. Maybe it meant I was worldly; maybe it explained why I was never afraid of the unknown; or afraid when I saw spirits. Maybe it is why I have an uncanny ability to connect with most everyone I meet. Anyway, I made myself comfortable and the session began. I provided little information: I wanted her to tell me what she sensed. She used three different tarot decks and had me select from all three. The cards were strategically placed on the table and from there she began her reading.

One of the first things she asked was if I was an educator, teacher or coach. I told her I was but didn't tell her what I did or my profession. One of the next things she told me was I needed to write the book that was in my head. Seriously? Two people telling me this? *Honestly, ladies, I don't have a book in my head. What exactly do you want me to write about?!?* The session lasted about an hour. She hit the nail on the head with most other aspects about my health, life, marriage and career. She provided insight into upcoming events and gave me some things to ponder. Overall, I was very impressed, and I felt that some of what I was thinking and feeling had been validated. This was definitely money well spent.

The remainder of December was spent playing charades as I kept getting sick and losing my voice. It always seemed to happen when my body's immune system wasn't at 100 percent: This never stopped me from working or working out. LIFE WITHOUT LIMITS! I just resorted to sign language to get my point across.

THIRTY-THREE

MY CROHN'S TREATMENTS

I need to go back a few years and fill in some gaps about my health. During the summer of 2008, my gastroenterologist would no longer refill the prescriptions I was taking. He said it had been too many years since I had a colonoscopy and I needed to schedule an appointment. Maybe my medications needed to be reduced or increased. So as much fun as these tests are, I scheduled my appointment.

The day of my procedure, Mark drove me to the testing center. Everyone is always super nice as they know how each patient is so miserable. After being escorted back into the treatment center, I was asked to change and wait for the nurse to come in to insert my IV. I had a young nurse enter the room and begin the process. Now, remember, I have gone through this a time or two and I know how this is supposed to feel, and this time it hurt like hell. Actually I wanted to cold-cock the nurse it hurt so badly. It didn't feel like she inserted the needle correctly. I said something, but she assured me all was OK. I winced again as she attached the tubing, she assured me everything looked just fine. *Alright sweetie, we shall see about that.*

After a brief wait, I was wheeled back to the procedure room, to wait again while the nurses, anesthesiologist and other staff members do their thing. They try to make simple conversation, but all you are thinking is in a few minutes you are going to be looking at my butt and what if I didn't prep enough, what if I have an accident? I do not want to talk, so please stop asking me questions and trying to exchange pleasantries! I just want this to be over.

Next the staff instructs you to roll onto your side and the anesthesiologist says he is going to start the sedation, and that warmth will be felt throughout the body and to start counting backward from 100. OK: 100, 99, 98, 97, 96, 95, 94, 93, 92, 91, hello!!! I have done this before – I should have been out at 97! He looked at me, and I look back at him. I tell him, "I told the nurse who inserted the needle that it was not in right spot, but she assured me it was OK." Then we both looked at my arm, which had blown up to the size of an elephant's leg and was now totally numb. Yup, she missed the vein, so all the medicine had been going directly into my arm. After he repositioned the needle; I was out like a light. The doctor performed the procedure and I was wheeled back to the recovery area. When he came into the room to tell me the results, I was totally taken by surprise. He said there were over 13 areas of inflammation and ulcerations. He was totally amazed I was not complaining or hurting. Well, like I have said before, sometimes one just gets used to feeling a certain way and you go on with your life. If I hurt, then I just sucked it up and went about my daily business.

The doctor decided I needed to try some new therapies, as the maintenance drugs I was taking apparently weren't working. There were many new drugs on the market now and he suggested I begin with some monthly injections. I had three choices: The decision would be determined by what the insurance company was going to cover. Pretty sad we must base our lives, well-being and general health by what our insurance company will pay. How is it these drugs are so expensive? I mean, really, a couple thousand dollars per injection? Am I getting liquid gold?

The nurses told me there were assistance programs that would help cover the cost of what the insurance didn't pay. *Why the hell do I pay my premiums if the insurance company won't cover what ails me?* It's bad enough there are 10 general conditions/diseases most insurance companies consider uninsurable and Crohn's is one of them - right up there with AIDS and cancer. Meanwhile, I'm paying a premium that is larger than my house payment, because I have to have private insurance. Then I have to choose the plan with the highest deductible so my ridiculously high premium will be lower. Then, I still don't get coverage for my condition. Insurance is a sore subject!

Once the doctor and I determined which treatment to start with, the nurses got all the paperwork completed and helped get me set up with the assistance program. As soon I received clearance, my first injection was scheduled. There would be a series of injections over a period of a few months. Then we would wait and see how I felt. Well, to begin with, I didn't feel badly?!? So I'm sure I'm not going to go, *"Ooh Ooh... I feel better now!"* On top of the injections, I still needed to take the maintenance medications. This meant I still needed to pay out of pocket for those along with the new bills I would incur from the injections.

A few months went by, and I didn't feel any better or worse. The only way the doc was able to tell how I was doing was from the results of my blood draws.

My inflammatory levels were the same, which meant the drug was not working. He suggested I try the other injection drug. OK, no problem, but then I needed to go through another assistance program enrollment, as this drug was made by a different manufacturer. Great! Thanks! Again, we went through the paperwork process, received approval and tried the next medication. After a series of injections and lab work, my inflammation markers still weren't improving. *Why in the hell won't my body respond to this new medication?* I knew I couldn't go back on the original infusion I got many years ago, because once one stops taking it, the body builds up antibodies so taking it again would result in anaphylactic shock!

The doctor increased my maintenance medications and added a new one, and told me to give it a few months: he would redraw my blood and we would take it from there. Basically, I spent the last 12 months driving back and forth to St. Louis to get an injection, which took all of 10 minutes, only to find out one year later that wasn't the answer. Well, then what was the answer? I am doing everything in MY power to help myself. I am a vegan, I strength-train and do my cardio on a daily basis; I drink only on occasion; I drink plenty of water; I follow gluten-free guidelines; I do not smoke; I do not do drugs; I do not eat fast food. What else is there? The doctor knew of a new experimental research study in the area and suggested I see if I qualified. He provided me with all the contact information and told me to let him know if I was accepted into the study.

    I have never been in a research study before and really was not sure what to expect. Basically one is a human guinea pig as they don't know what the drug will do to you, or what are the long-term effects. I'm sure you have seen the ads and commercials on TV: earn money for your participation in this or that study. I never dreamed in a million years I would actually be a candidate for one. I picked up the phone and made the call. We set up a time to meet and complete the applications. The head nurse needed my health history too, and I promptly gave her my gastroenterologist's number, as my health file was bigger than a box of reamed paper. There were three main criteria I needed to meet and I met two of the three, but there was still a way to be accepted into the study. However, it involved another colonoscopy! *Oh, good grief! Again?* But if I was to get into this study that is what I had to do, and so I did it. Lo and behold after a year of injections and maintenance medications, my gut was still as inflamed and ulcerated as it had been before. These sad, but obvious results were acceptable, and I was granted access into the study.

At this point I really was not too concerned about all the potential symptoms I might experience, I just wanted to feel better and not have the urgency to use the bathroom 10-20 times a day. Even though this symptom is something one gets used to, I didn't like it nor did it make my life easy. It was what it was.

Before the study actually began, I was given multiple forms to complete. I was instructed to read the protocol; I was instructed to initial the bottom of every page. I was then told I would need to call in to an automated system every evening and answer a set of questions, and I needed to do this for one full year. Wow! OK, no problem I'll do it if that is what it takes.

This study was to test a new medication that was site-specific. This means it targets only the areas that are of concern, unlike the other injections I received where the medication targeted the entire colon. The study was to begin in December and it was going to be offered nationally as well as internationally. After one-and-a-half years, I found out I was the first to enter the study in the United States.

There were three possible scenarios for the study during the first year: I could receive a placebo; I could receive the medication at every visit; or I could receive the medication at every other visit. Because it was a double blind study the head research nurse didn't even know what I was getting. But one would imagine that if I was the first participant, I would be getting the actual medication, right? But I won't know until the study is officially closed.

In December 2008, I began receiving the medication via infusions every four weeks. The visit was not bad; it took about two hours out of my day between the drive to and from, and the actual infusion time. It was the nightly call that sucked. I dialed in to an automated system that asked questions, which one couldn't answer until it gave you all the possible choices. Why wasn't this done online? It would literally take me two minutes to complete online, but no, I had to sit on the phone for about seven minutes every night answering the same flippin' questions. I even had to do this when I went on vacation! After the initial year, the calls ended.

Honestly, I was feeling better, my routine improved and my arthritis did feel better. Another year passed and my overall health was better than fair. I had my bad days - I had my laryngitis - and I had my good days. The study required frequent blood draws and each time my levels were skewed in some way. My iron was usually low and my hemoglobin was always two to three points lower than the norm. A low iron and hemoglobin level means my red blood cells weren't big enough or there weren't enough red blood cells to carry oxygen to the body, which means one gets tired and sluggish. Well, sluggish isn't in my vocabulary, so I just went about my daily business. I tried to supplement with some over-the-counter iron pills, but they just made things worse. I tried to eat as many green leafy vegetables and beans as I could because this lady was not eating any animal or organ meats!

Year two turned into year three and the study reached its target-end date. But the researchers decided they wanted to extend the study so they could obtain long-term data. This meant if I wanted to, I could remain in the study for an additional five years. Since the last few months had brought about some old aches and pains, which meant I was starting to have a flare-up, I decided that staying in the study would be a good thing. And they decided to start me on some oral medications as well. I thought it was in my best interest to continue in the study and I signed on for another five years.

I often wonder - when I am asked the same routine questions (Is your eyesight getting worse? Are you more tired than usual? Do you have trouble staying focused?) at each visit - if things are changing because I'm getting older or were they related to the effects of the study medication. My eyesight has gotten worse, considerably worse actually, but is it related to the medication? Age? How will we know? We won't!

I hate answering subjective questions as everyone has such a different level of tolerance for pain. I have a very high threshold for pain, so my answer is going to be very different from someone who is a big weenie! I have never let a little ache or pain get in the way of doing something; I always try to be strong and tough and put on a game face. If I believe that it is LIFE WITHOUT LIMITS, I can't very well let a little ache and pain get in my way of reaching a goal.

Sure my arthritis gives me fits some days. Related to medication? Weather? Age? What if I didn't exercise, would the arthritis be worse? Good question. Again, I hate subjective questions. But I did learn if I ever answer, "Yes", to the question: "Are you experiencing any dizziness or ability to concentrate?" I get a free spinal tap! So even if I am, my answer will be a resounding NO!

I look at my participation in the study as my way to further research and help others; even though I might experience some unknowns, hiccups and potential long-term issues, I am doing this because it is helping me and might help others as well. I am getting free healthcare to some extent. And while I may have my up's and down's, good days and not so good days, overall, I feel lucky to be involved in this study.

THIRTY-FOUR

FIVE-YEAR ANNIVERSARY

Wow, I cannot believe it has been five years since I opened my private practice. Where has the time gone? My lease was up for renewal and I needed to decide if I wanted to sign on for another five years. The answer seemed easy, but stopping to consider this commitment made me feel restless and unsure. Ultimately I did sign, but really, who knows what the next few years would hold.

With the bodybuilding on hold, I turned my focus toward running. I was running a lot of miles and entering a lot of races. I noticed that most events raised money for a certain cause. This made me stop and think. If I am running all these races, why not run and raise money for a cause near and dear to my heart?

I discovered the Crohn's Colitis Foundation of America's (CCFA) Midwest chapter was located right here in St. Louis and that they hosted many fundraising events the next of which was the Napa to Sonoma half-marathon in July. I immediately called to inquire; spoke with a chapter recruiter; and attended an informational session. I was hooked. This is perfect. I can do what I enjoy (run), all while raising money for the organization that might someday find a cure for this disease that I have relentlessly endured for the last 30 years!

I immediately signed up and became part of Team Challenge. I began planning my training schedule and raising money as I only had four months to prepare.

I attended as many Team Challenge group training runs as I could, but they typically were on Saturday mornings and those mornings were usually busy for me with trainings and consultations. I began to form friendships with others in the group and was amazed and in awe at the reasons for individuals' participation. I felt humbled to know that others would run for me and that made me run that much harder.

I had no troubles raising the specified amount of money - and actually went over and beyond my goal. Every client, friend, family member and business was extremely generous with his or her contributions. As a way of saying thanks, I had a race shirt made with all of my sponsors' names listed. It is actually the shirt I am wearing on the cover of this book.

The four months passed quickly and the day finally arrived for Team Challenge to depart. I was so happy to be a part of something so heart-warming and motivating. I can't even begin to explain the extent of the festivities we experienced while in Napa. There was a welcome party, pre-race banquet, early-bird breakfast, awards ceremony and lots games and wine at the after-race party. This was truly an event I will never forget. Witnessing so many runners, supporters, and spectators cheering for the sea of blue- and orange-clad athletes running through the winding roads of Napa Valley put a tear in my eye.

Our team leaders consisted of a manager, coach and a mentor. We had so much support and encouragement along this journey; one never felt like they were alone. I was so inspired by all the attention given to our group I wanted to sign up for another race, and if they would have me, I wanted to be a mentor.

The role of the mentor was to help, guide, motivate and be the team cheerleader. It was a perfect volunteer position for me. I completed the application and was accepted to be the mentor for the next event which was a half-marathon in...VEGAS!

CCFA and Team Challenge didn't waste any time beginning the next group of recruitment sessions. We ultimately ended up with 15 participants for this event. I did not waste any time introducing myself to each and every person to let him or her know I was here to help every step of the way. Even though my role was as a mentor, I still chose to raise money for the December Vegas event. This time it was a little more difficult so I approached my fund-raising efforts with contests and freebies, which worked well for those who donated and for me to reach my goal.

I continued with the day-to-day activities of my private practice trainings, nutritional consulting and other assorted seminars and talks, as well as adding these new mentoring duties into the mix.

Even though I was planning on running in the December event, I needed a more short-term goal, so I signed up for - not one but two - local half-marathons and a few 5K and 10K events, and before I knew it the summer and fall months flew by. One of the very few seasonal changes I did look forward to was the leaves changing colors. There is nothing more beautiful than a 75-year-old maple tree with leaves that have turned burnt yellow like the color of the burning sun. This unfortunately short-lived seasonal change only means one thing: Winter is around the corner. Seems the combination of the impending winter and turning the clocks back, sends me into a funk, which in turn sets off my Crohn's. I also realized my outdoor running would soon become treadmill running and that makes for long, monotonous training sessions.

I managed to keep my Crohn's under control until the beginning of November when the arthritis and gut pains appeared. I was not put on any additional medicine at the time; the doctors were going to see if the symptoms subsided when the Vegas event was over. I would like to blame the colder temperatures, but I am sure the additional races I signed up for didn't help. Still, I was hooked on running, beating my finish times and racking up the bling i.e., Finisher's Medals!

I really never had the desire to go to Vegas, unlike my mom and dad who had a little of the gambling bug in them. Vegas was not for me. I didn't like to stay up late; I have zero desire to eat from an "all-you-can-eat" buffet; and I am not a fan of loud casinos with lots of bells, whistles, clanging and yelling. Now, while I do enjoy my wine, I had no intention of drinking bottomless margaritas or other assorted drinks. And while people watching certainly was entertaining, the part that made me the saddest was seeing the showgirls and realizing I couldn't do that anymore.

Departure day finally arrived and the Team Challenge group was more than ecstatic. I was so proud of how much they improved in their running times and confidence levels. They were a motivated group and completely amazed, once again, when they saw that CCFA spared no expense at making Team Challenge feel like they were royalty. Vegas truly is a city that never sleeps. All the planned festivities were beyond subdued and the best part about this event is it is one of two times the city of Las Vegas shuts down The Strip. It was surreal to run down The Strip at night and see all the lights, hotels and neon, not to mention the thousands of spectators, Elvis' and other assorted impersonators cheering you on.

I once again met my fund-raising goal and was forever indebted to the generosity of those who supported me: the friendships I formed with other Vegas Team Challenge members still exist to this day.

Shortly after returning from Vegas my Crohn's was in full flare. It did not subside like we had hoped, and another round of steroids began. So the cycle repeats itself yet again. Pain, swelling, weight loss, lethargy, poor appetite, but I did have our annual winter vacation to look forward to and this year we were headed to Jamaica, Irie! Maybe a little RNR was just what mama needed.

THIRTY-FIVE

....

OH, THE THINGS CLIENTS SAY!

I am not going to lie, I wanted to rub-in the fact I was headed to a warm and sunny beach, but I didn't. I always enjoyed our winter get-a-ways: There is nothing better than digging your toes in the sand or feeling the heat of the sun on your skin, or not having to worry about cooking, cleaning or any other chore. It was a time to relax, rest and I used it as a time to reflect.

I realized how fortunate I was to have a thriving practice and how thankful I was that I completely love what I do. I love it because I am helping people become healthier; I am helping people who want to be helped; I am helping people by setting an example; and I am guiding, motivating and encouraging people every single day. People want to become healthier for so many reasons. The upcoming reunion, beach vacation, wedding, recent diagnosis of X, or turning the dreaded 50. Whatever their reason, they call upon professionals to help guide them and give them structure and accountability. Sure, they can turn to the internet for diets and workouts, and menus and meal plans, but have you ever just googled the word diet? Last time I did it, I got over 148,000,000 hits. What does that tell you? Everyone out there has the latest and greatest diet. They say you don't have to exercise, you don't have to modify your eating, you don't have to give up fast food, just drink this powder before every meal, pop this pill three times a day and you, too, can lose 10 pounds in four days. What the hell is that about? Don't worry. I'm not going to go into a rampage on statistics on obesity, but what I am going to do is remind you if it really were that simple don't you think we, as a society, would be healthy? People focus too much on counting calories, not chemicals!

Life isn't about being skinny; it is about being strong and fit, and that, my friend, comes in all shapes and sizes. Take runners, for example. Remember when I ran the Chicago half-marathon? I saw people who were tall, lean and lanky, short and round, some had long legs, and even some with prosthetic limbs. I have learned to never judge a person by their outward appearance (Unless it is a bodybuilding competition.)! I have the pleasure of training and working with men and women who are very strong though they might not look like it. Being skinny doesn't mean you eat like a bird or you eat fat-free food, or even that you are healthy: It means that is how you are made! Your DNA or genetics decides that for you.

Your metabolism is always at work and knows how to adjust when you are stressed, tired, sick, exercising or go on some crazy crash diet. The human body and the way it works has always amazed me. It always tries to save itself by creating a homeostasis or a balance. Otherwise it would be subjected to all the things we try to do to it. For example; diet, eat 500 calories a day, go on a juice fast, cleanse, inject something into it, detoxify it, run marathons, overeat, smoke, drink alcohol, do drugs, and the list could go on and on.

Even though it has been one of the hardest things for me to do, I have learned over the years my body needs rest days (from exercising). Since I was young it was always dance classes, rehearsals or performing. I did something every single day. That was how I got better - I practiced. To not do something, to me, was wrong! I needed to move each and every day; however, as I have gotten older and my goals have changed, I now train for events vs. practice.

It doesn't sound like it is different, but it is. Training means to push oneself to improve something; speed, time, distance, cardiorespiratory endurance, VO2max etc., something that gives measurable results. Practice means doing the same move over and over until it is perfected. I have found that rest days allowed my body to recover so by my next training session my body was ready to be pushed past its limit once again. Sure, I have and get aches and pains, but I always ask myself these questions: *"Do I hurt? Can I keep going? Is it life threatening?"* Sure something likely hurts; of course I can keep going - I may not want to but I can; and unless I have injured myself, it likely isn't life threatening. If you don't learn to push yourself; NO one will or can do it for you. Nobody can push you better than you. Your mind is usually what is telling you to stop or rest, or go faster, or slower. It is always our mind - always a mental game! When I am running and I want to quit, I ask myself; *"Can I give more?"* - and the answer is usually, *"Yes!"*

The same rules and principles apply to eating. Back in the day, people ate because they were hungry. Your belly growled and you fed it. Think as far back as the caveman or as recently as your grandparents: They worked for their food. They planted and reaped, and cooked their food. The idea and notion of a fast-food restaurant was no where in sight. There weren't any manufacturing plants where food was created and there weren't any chemical additives or added preservatives to keep food fresh. They ate real food. But as the population grew the supply couldn't keep up with the demand and the beginning of processed, and fast food industry was born.

I'm pretty sure our body and our DNA was not designed to process red dye #3, high fructose corn syrup, emulsifiers or stabilizers. I'm pretty sure our stomachs weren't designed to hold a triple cheeseburger, large fry and a coke. We have gone from a society that worked for their food to a society that can have food delivered to their front door. We have gone from eating real food to eating fake food. What we are eating these days isn't food! A candy-corn flavored Oreo – really?! And we wonder why there are such high rates of obesity, diabetes and heart disease.

People often call me with despair or urgency in their voice. They want help! They want help NOW! They are ready to make the changes! This time they are going to stick to the plan.

After we have our initial consultation and I learn about where they have been and where they want to go, I have a better understanding of how to help them. But often what I find isn't that their motivation is gone; it is their dedication to the fact the changes they need to make are hard, challenging and life-long. This concept overwhelms most. The thought of doing something – forever - is daunting. It is just as easy to make the right choice, as it is the wrong one.

I often use myself as an example as to why the changes I have made have helped me so much. I can't very well be a good role model or example to others if I don't follow my own advice. The difference is that I don't veer from my diet, because the alternative for me is pain and discomfort. That isn't the case for most. Do I miss chocolate cake? Maybe. Do I miss cheese? Likely. Would I like to be able to go out to eat and actually eat something instead of just sit there? Yes! But for me the alternative is pain, bloating, gas, cramps and usually the dreaded 'D' word. I would much rather eat what I know is *safe* than run the risk of any or all of the above. It just isn't worth it!

All I can do when someone comes in seeking help is to guide him or her and encourage them the best way I know. For some I use kid gloves, for others scare tactics, and yet others nothing short of a baseball bat (well, I really don't use that, but you get the idea).

The people I work with don't always learn from me - often I learn from them - whether it is a funny saying, way of learning a move or a new perspective on something. The following are a few of the things people have said to me over the last several years:

"Oh, look at the time!"

"What did I ever do to you?"

"Oh, you mean like having tea?"

"Is it your mission to make teenagers cry?"

"You mean squat like I'm trying to avoid sitting on the port-a-potty?"
When I ask, "What are you thinking about? The answer was: "I'm rowing to Warren on the island!"
"You mean pick the kettle-bells up like they are luggage?"
"When was the last time you checked to see if the AED worked?"
"I think I need to hydrate!"
"You want me to eat what?"
"Vodka is made with potatoes, doesn't that count?"
"I took the skin (chicken skin) off!"
"You will only see me running if there is a bear chasing my ass!"
"I'm allergic to exercise."
"But it was only 29 cents more to super-size it!"
"I really don't think my body is supposed to bend like that!"
"I thought you were my friend!"
"I don't like coming here, but always feel better when I'm done."
"I was trying to be good!"
"But it was sugar-free, low-fat or low-calorie!'"
"I can't lift that much weight." (I'm pretty sure your purse weighs more than a five-pound dumbbell)
"My dog ate a rabbit and I had to take him to the vet."

Over the years I have formed phenomenal relationships with the individuals I work with. I often hate to use the word client, because I feel as though we are more than that. I feel as though everyone is my friend, some almost like family. I have seen individuals get married, divorced, change jobs, have babies, have more babies. I have watched their children grow and graduate; and I have been to their parents' funerals. I know their pet-peeves, I know which buttons to push to set them off, I know who will always be late for an appointment and what their favorite TV shows are. I know what their favorite foods are and thanks to social media I can follow them daily (whether they want me to or not). These are the connections that help me to better help them. But they are also the connections that give me too much information. By that I mean, it makes me sad when sad things happen to them, or I know so much about them I want to try every approach to help them reach their goal. I have always encouraged individuals I work with to ask questions, send me pictures of the food they eat, text me images of their heart rate monitor when they are finished with their workout. I always want to be available and there for them when they need help, motivation and direction. But these are also the same reasons that made it so very, very hard for me to think that maybe it was time for a change.

THIRTY-SIX

....

WHERE DO I GO FROM HERE?

Well, the sun and fun of Jamaica was short lived. We returned home to cold and snowy weather, and I seemed to have brought a flu bug home with me. There was no hope of showing off my dark bronzed tan; instead I spent the next week lying on the couch thinking I might die. I didn't move except to get up and use the bathroom if that tells you anything. I did not care if I ran, worked out or even showered! Eventually I got better, but in the meantime I was unable to work toward one of the three 2013 goals I set for myself. The first and most important goal was to run 2013 miles, which averaged out to be roughly 5.5 miles per day: It seemed challenging, but doable. I also wanted to do more volunteer work so I signed up to be a driver for a local non-for profit agency, and I wanted to collect used shoe items that could be sent to third-world countries. But between the flu and the fact that Mother Nature was fighting us tooth and nail with a harsh winter, all I found myself wanting to do was stay home and stay warm. This combination coupled with the fact I am an individual who is in constant need of goals and new adventures, put me in quite the mental funk.

As I alluded to previously, I was thinking about trying a new business venture or a career change. One might think, why are you considering closing a successful private practice? Honestly, I didn't know what I wanted to do. I did know the success of my practice is something for which I will be eternally grateful. I also knew my health had been suffering; I think as a result of taking everyone's problems to heart. I was always in search of new approaches for clients when what we were doing was not working. So the last thing I wanted to do was disappoint anyone or not be their rock. But what I was beginning to realize was my desire to be their rock was what was affecting my health.

Seven years was the longest time I had stayed with one venture. So this was victorious on many levels. As I look back I realize the relentless miles I logged was a way for me to work through my dilemma; almost like I was trying to run away from the inevitable. And if my logbook is accurate I ran on average, 30-50 miles - PER

WEEK! Now mind you I was training for many events, my first marathon included, and I had that 2013 running goal.

All these miles are hard on anyone's body, let alone one that is compromised and weakened from a disease like Crohn's. February and March came and went, and I found my Crohn's decided to continue to rear its ugly head. But I didn't let it stop me from running my business or completing my training miles. I carried on with my daily commitments, NO EXCUSES!

The doctors finally decided I needed some intense therapy and prescribed steroids because at this point between being sick from the flu, and sick from a flare-up, I had lost a substantial amount of weight. Not to mention I am sure all the calories I was burning from running wasn't helping matters either. If you remember, steroids give me unwanted energy and take away my appetite, but they also take away the pain. So the doctors started me on a round of the magic pills. Yes, they did the trick, but not in time because at this point I had lost almost 20 percent of my body weight. I went from a healthy 115 pounds to 93 pounds. It happened gradually so I didn't really seem to notice. But the concerned remarks from friends and family made me stop and take a long hard look in the mirror. They made me realize I looked like a skeleton and I was bringing a lot of this on myself. However, my hardheaded, bound and determined personality continued to persist. I was not going to disappoint or let down anyone.

As April rolled around, a group of my local running buddies decided we should run the Lincoln Springfield half-marathon at the end of the month. It was advertised as a flat course, but what got me to sign up was the finisher's medal was a giant penny! Funny I have lived in Illinois for almost 20 years and never been to the states capital, so it was fun to run this race through the historic downtown area. The event promoters were right, the course was flat and I actually ran one of my fastest half-marathons.

With that race over, the marathon I had been training for was right around the corner. I was feeling much better due to the steroid therapy and was getting very excited to run this race. A long-time friend drove with me to Kentucky to keep me company and cheer me on. I was so proud of myself: I never missed a workout and I actually gave myself a sad face on my log sheet when I didn't run at the speed I wanted to achieve.

I remember the event well and even though it was chilly and drizzly, it was the best and most rewarding experience I have ever had. Who knew the feelings of awe, accomplishment and joy would be so overwhelming. Honestly, 26.2 miles really wasn't bad when you factor in the crowds cheering you on; the signs of encouragement along the way; the new sites to see; the people with whom you strike up a conversation while running. The time really did fly by.

There are a few pictures from this event of me running, which further reinforced my downward slide and weight loss. But I didn't want to stop running; I was so pumped from completing this marathon. Now I wanted to train so I could qualify to run the race of all races - the Boston Marathon. I had my new carrot: I was focused and my training schedule started immediately as the qualifying race was in November. The Boston Marathon is the only race that a runner must qualify for, which means, based on your gender and age, you need to complete the event in a specified time. Since I was 49, I needed to finish in four hours. So trainings were very specific in terms of time and distance. My training runs were actually much longer and at a faster pace. I also ran during the heat of the day, in the rain, on the school tracks, alone and with any willing body who wanted to join me. Basically I ran whenever I had the chance. Was I tired? Sure, but that was just part of the training, right? This structure had become my escape. I remained in total denial about the decision at hand and in turmoil over actually closing my practice.

I would always tell myself: *I will work through my dilemma during my long runs,* but honestly there were times when I could not put two thoughts together let alone make an important decision. Really, if you can't figure life's answers on a four-hour run, I'm pretty sure the answer isn't there.

It became apparent I was spending more time running than I was working. I was not seeking new clients or speaking opportunities. I was not motivated to move forward in any one way. I needed to make up my mind. What did I want to do? I can't keep carrying on like this because I cannot continue to have flare up's.

But I had signed another five-year lease, that meant I needed to find someone to take over the lease. Then I had the decision of whether to sell the business, or sell off the equipment. Do I really want someone else buying the business I worked so hard to create? It was my name and reputation they would also be buying and representing, so I did nothing short of continue to drag my feet. I did not want to make these decisions. Which meant my health would get worse, not to mention I was losing more weight and now it was costing me money to keep my doors open.

I decided I would start to look for other career options and maybe even apply for some real 9-5 jobs. But whom am I kidding? I don't work well with others and I am pretty sure I am not employable in the traditional 9-5 workday sense. I did come across a few positions I thought sounded interesting and I did go to a few interviews. I thought, if it is meant to be, then I will be offered a position and the decision will be made for me. But none of the positions I applied for came through, so I was back at square one.

I am not sure what made me do it: I'm not sure what light, bell or whistle went off, but I finally put it out there to the universe. Meaning, I finally verbalized to my clients, friends and family I was going to close my private practice and figure out what the next step in my life was going to be. I had to get a handle on my health and I had to get better. Everyone was extremely supportive and understood my decision. They all knew and realized I had everyone's best interest at heart, but they also knew I needed to take care of me.

The majority of the summer of 2013 was spent floating, boating or running. I was tired all the time, but I just attributed that to the fact that it was summer - it was warm - and I was running a lot of miles. I had completed the latest round of steroid treatments, I remained on my maintenance medications and the study infusions continued. I was more than halfway through my marathon training and I was starting to become frustrated as my times were getting slower not faster. What the heck? I knew my qualifying time was doable, but only doable if I did not have to stop for potty breaks or have any other issues. If I could just run, I would make it. This left little room for error (next year when I turn 50, I will get five more minutes tacked onto my qualifying time!). If the slower training times weren't stressing me out, I began to have minor injuries creeping in; a sore ankle here, an occasional throb in my hip there or not being able to get into a normal breathing pattern during runs. Any sane person would have seen the signs and stopped running, but NO, not Lorraine, I ignored the signs. I wasn't bleeding; I wasn't blue; it hurt, but wasn't life threatening; so ...one keeps going.

I thought the fact that I finally made the decision to close my practice would have made me feel better, but actually it made me feel worse. Now I was stressing about getting the space rented, selling the equipment and tying up loose ends. Funny how the old adages come back and bite you. The one that hit home for me was, If you don't take time for you and your health, the powers that be will take care of them for you. And lo and behold, my training came to a crashing halt about one month before race day. I did stop running but only because my body shut down. My arthritis was so bad. The aches and pains I was having won, and literally brought me to a screeching halt. I was so mad at my body and myself. But my body said, "*Lorraine, you are done! Stop running! I will not let you do this anymore!*" Trust me when I tell you there was never anyone more humbled, humiliated and defeated than me: To come so close to race day and then to have to verbalize to everyone that I was physically done? My mind was still in the game; it was my body I could not get to cooperate. Well, my LIFE WITHOUT LIMITS attitude found its limit! I needed to stop! And I did.

People say that one has to hit rock bottom before they can start recovering and getting better. This holds true for any addictive behavior whether it is alcohol, drugs, eating or exercise. I think I may have hit my rock bottom. Everyone was super supportive and they were all actually very worried about me. I was lucky if I weighed 90 pounds soaking wet. I was spent, wiped out, done! It was also becoming questionable as to whether they would keep me in the study. Wake up call number two, or was it three or four?

I decided my official closing date was going to be December 1st. I began advertising the space and I began the daunting process of selling the equipment. It only took about a month before I had someone to assume the lease and the majority of the equipment sold like hot cakes. November seemed to fly by, as there was so much administrative work to attend to. I was very happy there were not any hiccups in the closing process. December 1st was moving day and whatever equipment remained needed to be moved out. Well December 1st turned into the 2nd, 3rd, etc., and moving day actually became December 8th and wouldn't you know it, it snowed. How fitting since it snowed the day we moved in. Mark was on his own as I was sick and not able to help him heave-ho all the remaining items. I remember him continually saying something along the lines of, "You owe me big time."

THIRTY-SEVEN

THE END OF MY BEST RUN

I'm not going to lie, I was sad when I turned in my keys. A very rewarding and fulfilling chapter of my career came to a close. It was time for me to take of me. I needed to put my health first. So again I find myself in uncharted territory. What do I do with my days, my free time, my life?

Mark and I did not go on our usual winter getaway; instead we took a trip to Atlanta. The winter of 2013/2014 was brutal. Some days I was thrilled not to have to leave the house; it was one of those winters where I just couldn't get warm. There were days when I did not even change out of my pj's.

I thought I would really enjoy the downtime, but what I found out was that I missed having appointments. I missed getting dressed to meet a client. I missed the banter and influx of information. All the things I thought I had too much of, now I didn't have any of - I was bored!

I did not have a professional direction and I did not have a training goal. I felt like I was floundering and I couldn't even run away my woes, because my body was so beaten up and my iron levels were so low. As you can guess, I was more frustrated than relaxed. All this downtime gave me plenty of time to reflect.

I have come to realize that tomorrow offers new possibilities; that sometimes all the suggestions that cross my radar happen for a reason and I don't have to act on every one. Now, don't get me wrong: I'm going to think about it; consider it; I'm going to see if I can make it work. I have also found if I have to work really hard at something, maybe the project, timing or partner was not right at that moment. Sometimes things don't happen because there is something bigger and better that is supposed to happen.

What I do know is I have been blessed to have found the perfect mate; blessed by having the most amazing daughter; been able to do what I love (dance, educate, inspire); and while I do have health issues, I guess it could always be worse.

My final words to you: Life will throw you curve balls - it is all a matter of whether you decide to let those times break you or whether you stand tall and make no excuses - LIFE WITHOUT LIMITS.

THIRTY-EIGHT

THE CHAPTER I JUST COULDN'T WRITE

Not really sure where to begin, but maybe at the end. I have yet to this day to figure out why my mom waited until I flew down to Florida so she could die on my watch. I can still see her lying there, sad and sick, sore and miserable. And I remember yelling to Daddy, "Mom's not breathing!" Why did she pick me? Why wait until I'm in the room; why not when Daddy was there? Why did I have to witness this? After 21 years, I still don't have an answer.

Growing up with two very Catholic parents, you didn't talk about the birds and bees, you didn't share you medical ailments, you didn't air your dirty laundry, you didn't talk about money and you certainly didn't talk about death. Both of my parents were raised Catholic and were very devoted to their faith, and going to church. That was OK. I never questioned their beliefs; they were their beliefs and everyone is entitled to decide what makes them tick. But sometimes you wonder if there is such a greater good or God, then why was MY mom so sick? Why did she have breast cancer and have a mastectomy? Why did she have arthritis so badly she couldn't move her arms? If you prayed to feel better - and she did pray - then why didn't she get better? This is exactly why I have not written this chapter. I'll be back when I dry my eyes.

OK, birds and bees: I learned what I needed to know from my friends or books. Sex was a no-no conversation. Funny if you think about it, Catholics are known for having big families with lots of kids, maybe they should have talked more about sex, birth control or abstinence - just sayin'.

As for medical issues, well, I remember when daddy had his heart attack: The paramedics rushed him by ambulance to the hospital and placed a stint in one of his arteries. I think he had high blood pressure, but otherwise I didn't know much about Daddy's health when I was growing up. He was Army Airborne, then a bartender and finally ended up working for the U.S. Postal Service for 30-plus years lifting heavy boxes and packages: He worked in the yard and tinkered on things. He was a strong, hard worker. I never pictured him as being weak, frail or unhealthy. Maybe all the years of his three-pack-a-day habit of cigarette smoking, when he was a bartender for the Lago Mar Hotel in Fort Lauderdale, finally caught up with him.

As for Mom, I remember she was diagnosed with breast cancer when I was in the second grade. We used to play this game where she would lay on the floor with her legs in the air, and I would put my belly on her feet and pretend I was an airplane. I also remember falling once and landing on her chest, I thought for years I caused her breast cancer, that my fall triggered something that made her sick. I don't remember her surgery, but I remember her recovery and the way she had to do her physical therapy exercises using the louvered closet doors to increase her range of motion. I also remember the boob she kept in a box on the top shelf of her closet and the huge bra she had to use to support the boob, or to be politically correct, her prosthetic breast. I clearly remember the scar on her chest as it looked like someone had taken a flat iron and placed it on her chest and left it there until her breast melted away. The scar was a perfect looking triangle. I guess that is how they did things back in the early '70s. I also remember mom having other medical issues, but we never really talked about them - she was strong-willed and proud.

I know now she likely suffered quite a bit. I guess that is from whom I get my strength.

I never heard my mom or dad once talk about money. I know Daddy brought home his paycheck from the post office and gave it to Mom every week. I guess she handled the bills, although now that I think about it, I don't think I ever saw her actually write a check. I had no idea how much money Daddy made; I had no idea whether they had to pay the IRS or if they got a refund. I really was clueless! I do know I never wanted for anything. We always had food (and wine) on the table. We often went out for dinner and I always had new clothes. I do know they spent a small fortune on my dancing attire/costumes, etc., and the money for gas, too. I also remember getting a car for my 16th birthday. It was a white Fiat. Daddy had the seat covers redone in a black and white checkerboard pattern. They looked so cool! I loved that car! Even though I didn't know about our financial situation, I guess all was well.

Mom did work every now and then. I believe she said it was her mad-money. She worked at a dress store in the Pompano mall a few hours a week. Sherril Square was the name of the store if I remember correctly. I can't seem to remember any other job she had. I guess her main job was me!

LIFE WITHOUT LIMITS

We both loved to play cards and I learned all the games. Actually now that I think about it, Mom really did like to gamble. I'll say that loosely. She loved her Bingo and she and Daddy loved to go to the Palm Beach Kennel Cub, and bet on the dogs. They bought the racing program at the local drug store and Mom would look at each page, examine all the dogs in a race, and then strategically assign them numbers according to how many times that dog won, placed or showed. She was methodical and very precise in her calculations. She not only had this scientific method; she also used to pick the dog that pee'ed on his or her way to the starting gate. So much for precision! I think all in all - they likely broke even, but then again I had no clue. I also remember Mom and Dad going to Vegas. Can't tell you if they went alone, for a special occasion; I can't even come up with a year, but I do remember Mom came home with black fingers from the coins she put into the slot machines. Today you push a button. Back then you got to insert the coin and pull the handle. Again, no clue if they won or lost or broke even, but I am sure they both had a great time.

LORRAINE HUNTLEY

THIRTY-NINE

....

CROHN'S DISEASE, DEFINING & MANAGING

It is beyond the scope and intent of this book to fully explain all the causes, complications, treatment options and modifications there are for Crohn's disease. I do want to provide some generalized objectives and recommendations for you, and also share what has worked for me. For those who are unfamiliar with Crohn's disease, it is named after the man, Dr. Burrill B. Crohn, who first described it in 1932.

Defined: Crohn's disease is a chronic inflammatory condition of the gastrointestinal tract that belongs with a group of conditions known as inflammatory bowel disease (IBD), but it is not to be confused with other inflammatory bowel conditions such as ulcerative colitis (UC), enteritis or irritable bowel syndrome (IBS).

Describing:
- Location: Inflammation may occur anywhere along the digestive track
- Inflammation occurs in patches
- Pain: Commonly experienced in the lower right portion of the abdomen
- Appearance: Colon wall may become thickened and have a rough appearance; Ulcers along the GI track are deep and may extend into all the layers of bowel walls
- Bleeding: Bleeding from the rectum during bowel movements in not uncommon

Common Symptoms:
- Abdominal pain, cramping
- Intestinal bleeding
- Bowel narrowing
- Malabsorption
- Fever
- Persistent or recurrent diarrhea
- Joint pain
- Decreased appetite, Weight loss
- Nausea and vomiting
- Anemia
- Ulcers, Fistulas, Abscesses

Other possible symptoms:
- Erythema nodosum (raised red nodules/lumps) primarily seen on the shins
- Eye inflammation
- Delayed growth or sexual development
- Colon cancer

Diagnosis and Testing:
- Blood tests
- Stool samples
- Colonoscopy
- Sigmoidoscopy
- Barium enema
- CT scans/MRI

Medical Interventions:
- Medications such as:
    - Anti-inflammatory drugs/Corticosteroids
    - Immune system suppressors
    - Antibiotics
    - Pain reliever

Surgical Interventions:
- Removal of infected area
- Strictureplasty
- Ileostomy

Dietary Interventions:

- Dietary modifications - develop a food plan that will manage symptoms during acute phases of a flare-up; AND learn how to incorporate a healthy plan to promote recovery and during remission
- Iron, calcium, B12 supplementation
- Probiotics, Fish-Oils

It would be difficult for me to discuss medication therapies, as there are so many options available. Likely if you have Crohn's or know someone who does, one might discover there are multiple medications taken throughout the day that work in unison to achieve relief and/or a reduction in discomfort. And as you have read, I have taken my fair share of various medications, in various quantities over the years.

Since I have been fortunate to date and have not required any surgery, I would prefer to take this time and elaborate on the dietary and nutritional concerns associated with this disease. Through my years of personal experience, education and counseling, I believe I have the most information to share in this area. But one must remember there is no one single diet or plan that will work for everyone with Crohn's. Dietary recommendations must be tailored specifically for the individual - and may vary as the individual ages and/or the disease progresses or goes into remission.

Maintaining proper nutrition is extremely important in the management of a chronic disease such as Crohn's. Abdominal pain, reduced appetite, weight loss, diarrhea and bleeding can rob the body of fluids, minerals and electrolytes, which are vital nutrients needed for proper balance and body function.

That does not mean one must eat certain foods or avoid others, but there may be times when food modifications, especially during a flare, will help one recover more quickly.

One may find it helpful to keep a food journal to discover a correlation between what is eaten and the symptoms experienced. And while there is no one specific food that will worsen the inflammation of Crohn's; certain foods may aggravate symptoms.

A healthy diet should contain a variety of foods from all food groups, such as; proteins, grains, fruits, vegetables, dairy and fats. By trying to consume a variety of foods, one is reducing the risk for nutritional deficiencies. However, a supplement may be warranted and help fill a need in times of severe illness.

Finally, the following guidelines and suggestions are just that. Please consult with your physician, gastroenterologist and any other doctor whom you are under the care of.

Common dietary recommendations:

- Lactose-free: Limiting or avoiding dairy foods may help reduce symptoms such as diarrhea, gas, pain, and/or bloating. Often an enzyme product can be taken i.e. Lactaid that will help break down the lactase and help to manage discomfort if dairy must be or is consumed.

- Low fat: It is not uncommon to have difficulty digesting high or higher fat foods, especially during a time of a flare. The colon becomes unable to break down the fat, thus it passes quickly through the GI track causing or making diarrhea worse.

- Low fiber: If one has been experiencing a blockage or stricture (narrowing) then reducing the volume and density of foods consumed will help ease any pain and avoid over stimulation of the GI track.

- Low salt: When taking corticosteroids to reduce inflammation during a flare, it is suggested to avoid salt and/or processed foods as a way to reduce water retention.

- High calorie: During times of weight loss or growth delay, a high calorie option is encouraged to help prevent or reduce risk of malnutrition and vitamin/mineral deficiencies.

General dietary recommendations:
- Eat smaller meals at more frequent intervals (you will be better able to digest and absorb nutrients)
- Slow down when you eat, take small bites and chew food thoroughly
- Choose high quality, lean proteins (these will have less fat making them easier to digest)
- Bland, soft/er foods may be easier to tolerate (due to the lower fiber content)
- Avoid spicy foods, or consume as tolerated (higher acidic food may cause cramping and or pain)
- Reduce intake of greasy, high fat or fried foods (these foods will increase transit time in the GI tract causing diarrhea)
- Reduce intake of higher fiber foods such as nuts, raw vegetables, whole grains (these foods may be too hard to digest especially if one has any narrowed segments of the colon)
- Avoid carbonated beverages, these can cause an increase in gas production

- Restrict caffeine and consumption of sodas, especially when experiencing diarrhea, as caffeine can act as a laxative; the carbonation from soda can increase gas production and the sorbitol (or other artificial sweetener) can induce bouts of diarrhea
- If you are lactose intolerant, limit your intake of milks, ice creams, hard/soft cheese, yogurts and pudding
- Drink plenty of fluids, especially during times of a flare or when experiencing diarrhea so as to avoid dehydration
- Avoid alcohol at all times as medication interactions are possible
- Consider a multivitamin. Crohn's can interfere with one's ability to absorb nutrients and because one's diet may be limited, a multivitamin may be warranted.

Specific dietary recommendations:
- **Protein Options:** Be sure to limit consumption of breaded, processed or prepackaged protein items as these will be higher in fat and sodium
    - Lean cuts: chicken/turkey breast, beef sirloin, pork loin
    - Fish
    - Eggs and egg substitutes

- **Vegetables:** Cooked vs. raw may be easier to tolerate. However, one may wish to limit their intake of gas-producing cruciferous vegetables, such as:
    - Broccoli, cabbage, cauliflower, Brussels sprouts, onions, peppers

- **Legumes/Beans:** Higher fiber content and potential for gas production limit intake of:
    - Dried peas, beans, lentils

- **Fruits:** In general fruits should be well tolerated, but one may want to monitor intake of fruits with edible skins and seeds
    - Pears, peaches, berries
    - Dried fruits

- **Grains/Starches**: Select any or all that are tolerated. Due to the fiber content white vs brown or whole grain may not be toleraated during times of a flare
    - Rice, potatoes, yams, quinoa, cous-cous, buckwheat, barley, flours, oatmeal, crackers, cereals, breads, popcorn

- **Fats:** While pure sources are needed, processed fats are typically not tolerated well. Aim to include:
    - Vegetable oils, flax oil, coconut, peanut butter or other nut butters, avocado, mayonnaise, butter, oil and vinegar salad dressings

  Aim to avoid:
    - Fried foods, high fat meats/proteins, skin on poultry, margarines, processed snacks

- **Fiber:** Know when to avoid, but try to include, higher fiber foods when symptoms are under control. Be sure to consume small quantities:
    - Whole grain bread, bagels, buns. pasta, barley, corn, brown rice, quinoa
    - Bran cereals
    - Berries, apples, pears, peaches
    - Dried fruits
    - Beans and legumes
    - Green leafy and/or cruciferous vegetables

- **Vitamins and Supplements:** Depending on the complexity of one's disease, medications, lifestyle, additional medical concerns, some alternative therapies might be warranted:

-MCT oils (medium chain triglycerides/fatty acids) these are broken down making them readily available for digestion, absorption and utilization
- Multi-vitamins
- Iron and/or calcium supplements
- Elemental (predigested) drinks - these will give one's gut a rest while provided a wealth of nutrition
- Pre- Pro- Biotics - such as psyllium or live active lactobacilus yogurts
- Fish and Flaxseed oils

Alternative Therapies:
Smoking cessation
Stress
Lifestyle
Exercise

Alternative dietary therapies:
Gluten-free, Dairy-free, Vegetarian, Vegan

References and recommended readings

Crohn's & Colitis Foundation of America. Diet and nutrition.
Available at:
http://www.ccfa.org/info/diet?LMI=4.2
Accessed August 17, 2014

National Digestive Diseases Information Clearinghouse (NDDIC). Crohn's disease.
Available at:
http://digestive.niddk.nih.gov/ddiseases/pubs/crohns/index.htm
Accessed August 17, 2014

National Digestive Diseases Information Clearinghouse (NDDIC). Inflammatory bowel disease (IBD).
Available at:
http://digestive.niddk.nih.gov/ddiseases/topics/IBD.asp
Accessed August 17, 2014

Tsang G. Inflammatory bowel disease IBD diet (Crohn's diet).
Available at: http://www.healthcastle.com/ibd-diet.shtml
Accessed August 17, 2014

ACKNOWLEDGEMENTS

Any project is likely the result of many people's input, help and guidance and this book is no different. While the majority of this book was written at my kitchen table one summer when I was having a flare-up - it wouldn't be without the experience and memories of my past that helped me put pen to paper.

While I don't have any publicist or literary agents to thank, I do have my family and friends to send a heartfelt, sincere, grateful and humble thank you to. So many people have played a role in helping me achieve success that I am not sure where to begin but with a giant THANK YOU!.

My family has always supported me, my dreams, and my vision - without them none of what I have accomplished would have been possible. My teachers (school, modeling, and dance) instilled in me the drive, dedication, determination and motivation to see a project to its completion. My friends have always thought I was crazy and relentless in my pursuit of goals and carrots, it is with their open-eyed expectation that I persisted to see each and every venture I took on to completion. My clients made me realize that what I do has an impact on others and that I can and do make a difference in their lives even though I may not see it that way.

I am indebted to so many people who helped, offered advice, traded services and took me under their wing to help me bring this book to the masses. You know who you are and I am so very fortunate and blessed to have you in my life and that our paths have crossed.

I am most thankful, grateful and humbled to have found my soul mate who never once questioned my actions or motives, who stood by me every step of the often bumpy way. I am equally thankful, blessed and grateful to have the most amazing daughter whose big green eyes and bright smile always light up the room. Sometimes I wonder where she gets her endearing and warm-hearted personality, as I don't possess those warm fuzzy qualities like she does.

My goal for this book was to show that anything is possible, you can achieve your dreams and you can make a difference, but to also show that you can't do it alone. So THANK YOU one and all - you are the reason I do what I do and for that I am forever grateful.

LIFE WITHOUT LIMITS

Made in the USA
San Bernardino, CA
25 September 2014